The Healthy Smoothie Cookbook

Breakfast Smoothie, Body Cleansing Smoothies, Digestive Smoothies, Kid-Friendly Smoothies, Low-Fat Smoothies, Best Protein Smoothies, Easy to Make Weight loss Smoothies and etc.

Sheldon Miller

ISBN: 9781659429084

Table of Contents

Introduction

How to Get Started

Whether you are completely new to the world of Smoothies or just learning to explore new areas, the following sections of the book will help you to get a better understanding of the whole process of Smoothie making and help you to make the best Smoothies possible.

That being said, the first thing that you should know about Smoothie making are the components that you need to have in every drink.

So, whether you are only making your Smoothie for a quick snack or breakfast, always try to incorporate the following components:

- Liquid
- Fat
- Protein
- Fiber

Fat, Protein and Fiber will help you to enhance the power of your Smoothie to keep you energized throughout the day, and it will help you to stay full and satisfied.

On the other hand, it will also provide you with all the valuable macronutrients that you may need.

Just in case you are wondering, fruits, nuts, vegetables, seeds are all amazing sources of fiber, protein, and fat.

Additional sources of protein include protein powders, beans and also certain vegetables.

You can also find good healthy fats in oils, such as coconut oil, flax, hemp, chia or even olive oil, as well as ghee, nut/seed kinds of milk.

And lastly, we come to liquid. This is the base of your Smoothie that will help you to blend your smoothie easily and aid in digestion, circulation, hydration, skin health and even nutrient absorption, all while flushing out your body and detoxing it.

Water is possibly the cheapest and most convenient option when it comes to the liquid base, but you can always opt for coconut water, seed/nut milk or even 100% fruit juice.

How to Choose Your Blender

Many smoothie fanatics can have pretty strong opinions when it comes to choosing a blender. Talking to someone who blends religiously can be a little like talking to an automobile enthusiast who knows every detail of this year's supercars. What's the RPM of your blender motor? Polycarbonate container or glass? NSF certified? It can be a little daunting. and blenders come in every imaginable price range from ultra-cheap to uber-expensive.

High-end blenders like those by Blendtec, Ninja or Vitamix have a couple of major advantages: For one, the smoothie consistency (texture and taste) is far greater than a low- or mid-range blender option offers. Some other benefits of high-end blenders is that they wear out much slower than lower-priced blenders. This may not sound like the biggest selling point, but if you become a hardcore smoothie drinker, you will destroy blenders—even those in the $200–$300 range.

Typically, our experience is that a daily smoothie drinker will completely wear out a mid-range blender in one-and-a-half to two years. High-end blenders, on the other hand, come with three-year warranties.

So what should you do? Well, we believe in keeping this a completely personal choice. Don't feel like you have to spring for a $700 Vitamix off the bat; your everyday blender will do just fine. Start wherever you're comfortable but make sure you do your research. You want to buy a blender that's going to last for at least your first year of blending while keeping you healthy and safe.

Blenders can be nasty harbingers of bacteria if they're not cleaned often and properly, so make sure you're purchasing something that's not going to be too difficult to clean *daily*. Otherwise, you can run the risk of bacterial poisoning (including salmonella and E. coli) or worse. Also, make sure the container (including the blades) has been approved by the NSF, a third-party public health and safety organization that monitors the chemical composition of consumer products.

The main concern with blenders is to avoid having the plastic chemicals from cheap containers leach into your smoothies. If you get into the smoothie lifestyle (and have the available funds), we absolutely suggest upgrading to a Vitamix or Blendtec. They really do make a difference in your smoothie experience over the long run.

The Big Question, Frozen or Fresh?

If you enjoy adding a liquid base to your smoothies that doesn't come cheap or should only be consumed in moderation (like coconut water, coconut milk or pomegranate juice) and you don't use a lot of the base in each smoothie, save your fresh liquid ingredients for later by freezing them in an ice cube tray. Then add one or two cubes each time you blend a smoothie. Freezing your liquids will prevent them from spoiling or losing most of their nutritional content, and you'll end up with exciting flavors to punch up any blend.

In addition to saving good fresh produce from going bad, purchasing pre-packaged frozen fruits and vegetables is another excellent choice, especially if you're trying to save money.

Pre-packaged frozen fruits and veggies are often frozen by the grower before they have any time to degrade while sitting on the supermarket shelf, meaning they have almost the same nutritional content as if they were being eaten right off the plant. So you're consuming produce that is most likely much fresher than the "fresh" produce available in your local supermarkets, which have likely traveled thousands of miles (and up to a week since they were first picked).

In addition to being nutritionally rich, packaged frozen produce tends to be significantly cheaper than fresh, out-of-season produce and is available all year round, allowing you to enjoy your favorite berries, greens, and tropical fruits well into the cold winter months. Just remember to abide by the same rules as you would with fresh fruit. If it's a "Dirty" item, buy organic and always wash your frozen produce before you blend it.

Awesome Tips for Preparing Smoothies

While Smoothies are extremely easy and quick to prepare, sometimes, even if you have the best intention, luck does not stay with you and as a result, Smoothies do end up being unsavory. Or perhaps just simply due to lack of time, you aren't able to make one.

There are certain tips and tricks for situations such as these that will allow you to batch prep the ingredients for your Smoothies beforehand so that you are able to make your Smoothie in seconds after you wake up in the morning.

A good prep pathway includes:

- Make sure to properly wash, prep and measure out your ingredients before making smoothies.
- Make sure to add ingredients in a baggie jar, seal and label them with smoothie name.
- Once you are ready to sip, pour the liquid into a blender and dump all the contents of your bag into the blender and blend well.

The number of smoothie kits that you create will largely depend on the free space that you have in your freezer. But you can create at least 5 smoothie kits for your 4 days of the week, which should be a good place to start.

Another option is to fully blend your smoothie, make it and then just freeze it into cubes.

The Awesome 15 Superfoods for Smoothies

By now, you should have a pretty good idea of the awesomeness of Smoothies; however, there are actually a number of different foods, also known as "Superfoods" that will take the health factor of your Smoothies to the next level!

Some of the most common and awesome ones are as follows:

- Various berries
- Bananas
- Common nuts and seeds
- Dark leafy greens
- Yogurt and kefir
- Avocado
- Beets
- Oats
- Cinnamon
- Cacao, cocoa
- Ginger
- Turmeric
- Green tea and Matcha
- Pomegranate and Acai
- Chia seeds

The above 15 foods are high in all of the essential nutrients required by the human body. These ingredients are affordable and readily available in almost all grocery stores, and best of all, they add an amazing sense of flavor to your smoothie.

Common Mistakes to Avoid During Smoothie

If you are an amateur Smoothie artist, then it is very natural that you may face some difficulties early on. The following tips should help you deal with some of the most common issues:

- **Too Frothy:** If frothiness is the issue, try to add a little less liquid and not blend it for too long. Alternatively, you may withhold a portion of the liquid and gradually add it later on once the other half of the ingredients are properly blended. Keep in mind that when using base ingredients, such as Avocado, banana, etc., you won't need much liquid as they already have a fair amount of liquid on their own.
- **Too Runny:** If you find your Smoothie is too runny, reduce the amount of liquid and add more thickening ingredients.
- **Not sweet enough/tasty:** Add a bit of your desired natural sweetener; honey, dates or maple syrup are good options.
- **Too bitter:** An excellent way to tackle bitterness is to reduce the number of greens and add some fruits.
- **Not blending correctly:** If you find that you are unable to blend your ingredients properly, try to cut them into small pieces and add them to your blender. This usually solves the problem.

Some Common Smoothie Problems and Their Solutions

Even though the art of making Smoothies is so simple at its core, it is perfectly natural for individuals to face some sort of pitfalls, especially when you are working with limited time and ingredients. The Smoothie might end up being a bit slimy, chalky or even too slippery.

I have already talked about some of the common mistakes above, but let me dive into a few problems in a more detailed manner.

Too Sour Smoothie

When you are facing this problem, try to add a bit of natural sweetener to your Smoothie, such as honey, maple syrup, coconut sugar, dates, raisins, stevia. Try to start off with about ½ teaspoon, then add more as needed. A quarter of a banana sometimes helps too.

Too Sweet Smoothie

Try to add some freshly squeezed lemon or lime juice. For future reference, try to scale back on sweet fruits, add them in smaller amounts and add more if needed later.

Too Thin Smoothie

If you face this situation, add frozen fruit, avocado, chia seeds, flaxseeds, cooked pumpkin, frozen cauliflower, yogurt, nut butter, smoothie cubes from leftover smoothies and so on.

Too Thick Smoothie

If you see that your Smoothie is too thick, a good idea is to thin it with water, non-dairy milk, 100% juice. Add a little bit at a time, making sure that you don't overshoot and end up with a smoothie that's just too thin! Another good alternative is to add fresh fruit, instead of frozen. Fruits with high water content, such as grapes, cucumber, oranges, melon are good options.

Too Chunky Smoothie

If you find that your Smoothie is chunky, then a good option is to cut your vegetables into smaller pieces so that they can blend well. Try blending your greens with liquid first.

However, while doing this, make sure that you start off at a low speed and eventually increase to a higher speed. Also, whenever blending, make sure that you stop blender at intervals. If you see that your ingredients are getting stuck, simply stir the mixture, and add more liquid if needed.

Too Stringy Smoothie

If you find that your Smoothie is too stringy, this might be because some vegetables, such as celery, ginger, and stems of greens do not blend properly. This might be because your blender is not strong enough. If that's the case, try to eliminate your unblended bits and blend the stringier parts with water first, strain and then finally process them with the remaining ingredients.

Smoothie Feels Tasteless

If you find that your Smoothie is tasteless, you should keep in mind that the taste palette of every individual varies from one person to the next. However, it is good practice to always get the highest quality ingredients and the freshest as possible. Seasonal fruits and vegetables are the best options to go with. Another good idea is to add a bit of salt as it greatly helps to improve the flavor.

Hearty Blending Tips

Every chef or expert have their own method of creating the best Smoothie! But that doesn't mean there can't be a generalized method of creating an awesome Smoothie, right?

If you are a complete beginner, just follow the steps below to get the best Smoothie ever!

- First, add the liquid base
- Then add your herbs, veggies, greens
- Next, comes the fruit
- After that, add your nuts, seeds, butter, yogurt, etc.
- Then add spices and powders if using

This would be a good pathway to follow. However, there might be situations where you might need to add spices and powders after the liquid. For example, when you are using protein powder, it may not fully dissolve if it's added on top everything.

It also depends on what kind of machine you are using.

If you just have a regular and normal blender, it might need to blend the liquids with greens and veggies first, adding the other ingredients later to ensure that everything mixes well.

However, no matter what blender you use, it is always advisable to start off slow and then slowly keep increasing the speed as you progress.

If you go from "off" mode to "High" mode right away, then your ingredients will just likely fly around the blender and get stuck underneath.

Some people like to add ice to their Smoothies; you may do that if you want but be aware that it might water down the taste and balancing it out might be a little bit difficult.

As you keep practicing, you will eventually learn how to balance out the ingredients of your Smoothie and come out with the best possible flavor.

Healthy Ingredients

Some of the most awesome ingredients that you should know about include:

Macha

The maca root is native to the high mountains of Peru. It is a natural hormone balancer, providing health benefits to both men and women and is often recommended for fertility problems, sterility, and other sexual disorders. It's also a libido enhancer and helps to alleviate menopausal symptoms and painful menstrual symptoms. It's also a great source of energy; in addition to supporting your hormonal balance, it also restores and rejuvenates your adrenal glands to boost your energy and endurance.

COCONUT OIL

Coconut oil consists of 90 percent raw saturated fat and is a building block of every cell in the human body. It contains healthy, healing, medium-chain triglycerides (MCTs).

COCONUT WATER

Not only is coconut water sterile, but it also has the same electrolytic balance as human blood. In other words, drinking coconut water is a lot like giving yourself an IV. In fact, medics in the Pacific Theater of World War II would use coconut water as an emergency substitute for plasma during transfusions. I love drinking coconut water after a good work out!

RAW HONEY

When consumed unfiltered and 100 percent pure, honey is not only antibacterial—it's *full* of vitamins and minerals and is great for an energy boost. One-third of our total diet is dependent (directly or indirectly) on the honeybee and the dozens of plants it pollinates. As an ingredient, honey works to relieve irritation in your mouth and throat by forming a protective film, making it a great cough medicine. Honey can also be used in wound care: its antibacterial, antifungal and antioxidant properties make it great for treating wounds.

Interestingly, if you use local honey, it will likely contain pollen spores picked up by the bees from local plants, which, in turn, will introduce a small number of local allergens into your system. This can activate your immune system and, over time, will build up your natural immunities.

TURMERIC

This spice is popular as a healing root in Indonesia. It is a blood purifier and is beneficial for many different health conditions, ranging from cancer to Alzheimer's disease, hepatitis, and more. It equalizes blood sugar levels and is useful for easing stomach cramps and indigestion. Health studies have shown that turmeric can be three times more effective at easing the pain than aspirin.

WATERMELON

Watermelons are a natural diuretic and are great kidney and bladder cleansers. Rich in vitamin A and potassium, the melon also has a toning effect on digestion.

STRAWBERRIES

Strawberries are a mild diuretic and a natural painkiller—perfect for flushing out aches and pains from overexertion.

CELERY

Celery helps to curb one's cravings for sweets, and due to its high concentration of alkaline minerals (especially sodium), celery works to calm the nervous system.

BEETS

Beets are full of alkaline minerals like potassium and calcium and are great blood and liver cleansers. They help to build up the red corpuscles in the blood and are full of beta-carotene, calcium, fiber, folate, iron, potassium, protein, and Vitamins B6, C, and K. They are good for healing cancer, cardiovascular disease, dementia, high blood pressure, constipation, and are healthy for one's eyes and nerves.

APPLES

Apples help to regulate digestion and elimination (thanks to the natural digestive enzyme pepsin, which apples contain) as well as reducing cholesterol and enhancing mineral absorption. They are also a bowel regulator. Remember to store your apples in a cool location.

ORANGES

Oranges are high in vitamin C and calcium. Don't forget to eat the white part of the meat closest to the skin—it contains the bioflavonoids which enhance the body's absorption of Vitamin C.

CABBAGE

Eating cabbage can be helpful with digestion. Cabbage has a high fiber content, which helps to stimulate the digestive system while relieving constipation. Cabbage contains several cancer-fighting compounds, including lupeol, sinigrin, diindolylmethane (DIM) indole-3-cardinal (I3C) and sulforaphane, which may help to trigger enzyme defenses while inhibiting tumor growth. Cabbage is also one of the best natural remedies for stomach ulcers. A study at Stanford University School of Medicine found that fresh cabbage juice is very effective in treating peptic ulcers, due to its high glutamine content. This glutamine content is also believed to help those who are suffering from any type of inflammation.

Cabbage is also high in beta-carotene, which is great for your eyes, and its high vitamin C content strengthens the immune system. The lactic acid contained in cabbage helps to relieve muscle soreness.

PEAR

The quiet and unassuming pear is chock-full of vitamins A, B1, B2, C, folic acid, and niacin. They are also rich in many minerals, supplying the body with phosphorous, potassium, chlorine, iron, magnesium, sodium, sulfur, and a little calcium. But go easy on pear juice, as it does act as a diuretic and laxative.

CUCUMBER

Cucumbers are full of potassium and are valuable in balancing pressure (as well as helping gum and teeth afflictions). They are also great for fighting nail splitting, hair loss, and weight loss.

CARROTS

Carrots are full of magnesium and calcium, which help to strengthen your bones and teeth. Carrots contain Vitamins B, C, D, E, G, and K, and are rich in beta-carotene, a natural solvent for ulcers and cancerous conditions.

WHEATGRASS

On top of being a blood cleanser, wheatgrass also provides our daily requirement of chlorophyll, as well as more than 50 minerals and vitamins. Wheatgrass juice protects the lungs and blood from some of the air and water pollution.

PINEAPPLE

Pineapples contain bromelain, which is an active enzyme that serves as an effective anti-inflammatory agent.

LEMON

Lemons are amazing. Lemons (as well as limes, though to a lesser degree) are great for alkalizing the body. Lemons also neutralize the body and possess antiseptic properties. Many people start the day by mixing lemon juice and water together and drinking it; it has great digestive properties and can ease heartburn, bloating, and other digestive issues.

Did you know that if you drink a glass of lemon water every morning, it will actually kick-start your metabolism earlier? If you want to lose weight, start your day off by drinking lemon water. Also, if you drink hot lemon water, it can offer relief from cold and flu symptoms while providing Vitamin C. Lemon juice is also an all-natural skin cleanser.

Lemons are also full of calcium, magnesium, and potassium.

CORN

Corn contains ferulic acid, which is an anti-carcinogenic compound. It also contains fiber, potassium, and thiamine, as well as lutein (an antioxidant).

DATES

Dates contain calcium, fiber, iron, magnesium, manganese, niacin, polyphenols (anticancer compounds), as well as potassium and Vitamin B6. Who knew that the humble date could be so packed full of nutrients?

BANANAS

Bananas contain fiber, potassium, tryptophan, Vitamin B6, and Vitamin C. They are good for relieving stress, anxiety, depression, high blood pressure, blood sugar swings, muscles, even teething pain, and sleeplessness.

AVOCADO

Full of fiber, folate, magnesium, monounsaturated fat, potassium, steroids (cholesterol-lowering compounds, Vitamin B6, and Vitamin E, avocados are also noted as being good for your hair, high cholesterol, cardiovascular disease, cancer, blood sugar swings, and for alleviating insulin resistance.

BEAN SPROUTS

The first question people ask me when they find out I'm a vegetarian is, "Where do you get your protein?" Well, here's your answer, folks: sprouts are full of protein! Not only that but bean sprouts are full of calcium, fiber, iron, protein, and sulforaphane (an anti-cancer compound) and Vitamin C.

Chapter 1: Breakfast Smoothies

The Sunshine Offering

Serving: 2

Prep Time: 5 minutes

Ingredients:

- 3 cups fresh pineapple
- 2 tablespoons coconut, unsweetened flakes
- 2 cups spinach, fresh
- 1 ½ cups of almond milk
- ½ cup of coconut water

Directions:

1. Add all the listed ingredients to a blender

2. Blend on high until you have a smooth and creamy texture

3. Serve chilled and enjoy!

Nutritional Contents:

- Calories: 161
- Fat: 13g
- Carbohydrates: 11g
- Protein: 3g

Gentle Tropical Papaya Smoothie

Serving: 2

Prep Time: 5 minutes

Ingredients:

- ½ cup pineapple chunks
- 1 papaya, cut into chunks
- 1 cup fat-free plain yogurt
- 1 teaspoon coconut extract
- 1 teaspoon flaxseed
- ½ cup crushed ice

Directions:

1. Add all the listed ingredients to a blender
2. Blend on medium until smooth
3. Serve chilled and enjoy!

Nutritional Contents:

- Calories: 250
- Fat: 22g
- Carbohydrates: 13g
- Protein: 3g

Simple Vanilla Hemp

Serving: 1

Prep Time: 10 minutes

Ingredients:

- 4 cup leafy greens, kale and spinach
- 1 cup unsweetened hemp milk, vanilla
- ½ cup frozen blueberries, mixed
- 1 ½ tablespoons coconut oil, unrefined
- 1 tablespoon flaxseed
- 1 tablespoon almond butter
- 1 cup of water

Directions:

1. Add all the listed ingredients into your blender
2. Blend until smooth
3. Serve chilled and enjoy!

Nutritional Contents:

- Calories: 250
- Fat: 20g
- Carbohydrates: 10g
- Protein: 7g

The Ultimate Mocha Milk Shake

Serving: 1

Prep Time: 10 minutes

Ingredients:

- 1 cup brewed coffee, chilled
- 1 cup whole milk
- 2 tablespoons cocoa powder
- 1 tablespoon coconut oil
- 2 packs stevia

Directions:

1. Add listed ingredients to a blender
2. Blend until smooth
3. Serve chilled and enjoy!

Nutritional Contents:

- Calories: 293
- Fat: 23g
- Carbohydrates: 19g
- Protein: 10g

A Breakfast Egg Smoothie

Serving: 1

Prep Time: 10 minutes

Ingredients:

- 1-ounce egg substitute dry powder
- ½ cup coconut milk, unsweetened
- 4 tablespoons chia seeds
- ½ cup organic whole milk kefir, plain

Directions:

1. Add all the listed ingredients to a blender
2. Blend on high until smooth and creamy
3. Enjoy your smoothie!

Nutritional Contents:

- Calories: 266
- Fat: 17g
- Carbohydrates: 7g
- Protein: 22g

Tropical Flaxseed Smoothie

Serving: 2

Prep Time: 10 minutes

Ingredients:

- ½ cup pineapple
- 2 carrots
- 2 tablespoons flaxseeds
- 2 oranges, peeled
- 2 cups spinach
- 2 cups of water

Directions:

1. Add all the listed ingredients to a blender

2. Blend until you have a smooth and creamy texture

3. Serve chilled and enjoy!

Nutritional Contents:

- Calories: 151
- Fat: 2.5g
- Carbohydrates: 29.4g
- Protein: 4.1g

The Healthy Yogurt and Kale Delight

Serving: 1

Prep Time: 10 minutes

Ingredients:

- 1 cup baby kale greens
- 1 cup whole milk yogurt
- 1 tablespoon MCT oil
- 1 tablespoon sunflower seeds
- 1 cup of water
- 1 pack stevia

Directions:

1. Add listed ingredients to a blender

2. Blend until smooth and get a creamy texture

3. Serve chilled and enjoy!

Nutritional Contents:

- Calories: 329
- Fat: 26g
- Carbohydrates: 15g
- Protein: 11g

Cherry Berry Smoothie

Serving: 2

Prep Time: 10 minutes

Ingredients:

- 1 cup cherries
- 2 cups fresh kale
- 4 teaspoons honey
- 1 cup blueberries
- 2 cups almond milk

Directions:

4. Add all the listed ingredients to a blender
5. Blend until you have a smooth and creamy texture
6. Serve chilled and enjoy!

Nutritional Contents:

- Calories: 220
- Fat: 2.8g
- Carbohydrates: 47.7g
- Protein: 3.7g

Coffee Banana Smoothie

Serving: 4

Prep Time: 10 minutes

Ingredients:

- 2 cups brewed coffee, chilled
- 2 cups plain Greek yogurt, non-fat
- 2 tablespoons flaxseeds, ground
- 3 bananas, cut into chunks
- 4 teaspoons honey
- ½ teaspoon nutmeg, grated
- 1 teaspoon cinnamon, grounded
- 12 ice cubes

Directions:

1. Add all the listed ingredients to a blender
2. Blend until you have a smooth and creamy texture
3. Serve chilled and enjoy!

Nutritional Contents:

- Calories: 356
- Fat: 18.5g
- Carbohydrates: 44.5g
- Protein: 11.2g

Raw Chocolate Smoothie

Serving: 2

Prep Time: 10 minutes

Ingredients:

- 2 medium bananas
- 4 tablespoons peanut butter, raw
- 1 cup almond milk
- 3 tablespoons cocoa powder, raw
- 2 tablespoons honey, raw

Directions:

1. Add all the listed ingredients to a blender
2. Blend until you have a smooth and creamy texture
3. Serve chilled and enjoy!

Nutritional Contents:

- Calories: 217
- Fat: 2.8g
- Carbohydrates: 52.7g
- Protein: 3.4g

Chapter 2: Smoothies That Nourish Your Brain

Matcha Coconut Smoothie

Serving: 2

Prep Time: 5 minutes

Ingredients:

- 3 tablespoons white beans
- ½ teaspoon matcha green tea powder
- 1 whole banana, cubed
- 1 cup of frozen mango, chunked
- 2 kale leaves, torn
- 2 tablespoon coconut, shredded
- 1 cup of water

Directions:

1. Add all the listed ingredients to a blender
2. Blend on high until you have a smooth and creamy texture
3. Serve chilled and enjoy!

Nutritional Contents:

- Calories: 291
- Fat: 25g
- Carbohydrates: 18g
- Protein: 5g

Sweet Pea Smoothie

Serving: 2

Prep Time: 10 minutes

Ingredients:

- 2 cups sweet peas
- 1 cup blueberries
- 1 teaspoon honey
- 2 bananas
- 2 cups almond milk
- 2 tablespoons chia seeds

Directions:

1. Add all the listed ingredients to a blender

2. Blend until you have a smooth and creamy texture

3. Serve chilled and enjoy!

Nutritional Contents:

- Calories: 202
- Fat: 4.1g
- Carbohydrates: 38.4g
- Protein: 6.8g

The Gritty Coffee Shake

Serving: 1

Prep Time: 10 minutes

Ingredients:

- 2 cups strongly brewed coffee, chilled
- 1-ounce Macadamia Nuts
- 1 tablespoon chia seeds
- 1 tablespoon MCT oil
- 1-2 packets Stevia, optional

Directions:

1. Add all the listed ingredients to a blender
2. Blend on high until smooth and creamy
3. Enjoy your smoothie!

Nutritional Contents:

- Calories: 395
- Fat: 39g
- Carbohydrates: 11g
- Protein: 5.2g

Pomegranate, Tangerine and Ginger Smoothie

Serving: 2

Prep Time: 5 minutes

Ingredients:

- ½ cup pomegranate
- 1-inch ginger root, crushed
- 1 cup tangerine
- A pinch of Himalayan pink salt

Directions:

1. Toss the pomegranate, ginger roots and tangerine into your blender

2. Add a pinch of Himalayan salt

3. Serve chilled and enjoy!

Nutritional Contents:

- Calories: 121
- Fat: 6g
- Carbohydrates: 20g
- Protein: 4g

Berry Berry Smoothie

Serving: 4

Prep Time: 10 minutes

Ingredients:

- 2 bananas
- 3 cups blueberries, frozen
- 2 cups almond milk
- 2 tablespoons almond butter
- 2 handfuls ice

Directions:

1. Add all the listed ingredients to a blender

2. Blend until you have a smooth and creamy texture

3. Serve chilled and enjoy!

Nutritional Contents:

- Calories: 352
- Fat: 27g
- Carbohydrates: 41.5g
- Protein: 4.7g

Tropical Greens Smoothie

Serving: 2

Prep Time: 10 minutes

Ingredients:

- 2 cups mango chunks, frozen
- 3 coconut powder, unsweetened
- 2 cups leafy greens
- ½ cup lime juice
- 2 cups leafy greens
- 2 cups pineapple chunk, frozen

Directions:

1. Add all the listed ingredients to a blender
2. Blend until you have a smooth and creamy texture
3. Serve chilled and enjoy!

Nutritional Contents:

- Calories: 224
- Fat: 1.2g
- Carbohydrates: 54.2g
- Protein: 3.2g

The Blueberry Bliss

Serving: 1

Prep Time: 10 minutes

Ingredients:

- ¼ cup frozen blueberries, unsweetened
- 16 ounces unsweetened almond milk, vanilla
- 4 ounces heavy cream
- 1 scoop vanilla whey protein
- 1 pack stevia

Directions:

1. Add listed ingredients to a blender
2. Blend until you have a smooth and creamy texture
3. Serve chilled and enjoy!

Nutritional Contents:

- Calories: 302
- Fat: 25g
- Carbohydrates: 4g
- Protein: 15g

Grapefruit Spinach Smoothie

Serving: 2

Prep Time: 10 minutes

Ingredients:

- 2 bananas green, peeled and frozen
- 4 cups spinach, fresh or frozen
- 1 cup green tea, strongly brewed
- 2 grapefruits, peeled and frozen
- 2 cups pineapple, chopped and frozen
- ½ cup full-fat coconut milk, canned
- 4 tablespoons whey protein isolate
- 10 ice cubes

Directions:

1. Add all the listed ingredients to a blender
2. Blend until you have a smooth and creamy texture
3. Serve chilled and enjoy!

Nutritional Contents:

- Calories: 164
- Fat: 1.4g
- Carbohydrates: 36g
- Protein: 4.1g

Rosemary and Lemon Garden Smoothie

Serving: 1

Prep Time: 10 minutes

Ingredients:

- 1 stalk fresh rosemary
- 1 tablespoon lemon juice, fresh
- ½ cup whole milk yogurt
- 1 cup garden greens
- 1 tablespoon pepitas
- 1 tablespoon olive oil
- 1 tablespoon flaxseed, ground
- 1 pack stevia
- 1 ½ cups of water

Directions:

1. Add listed ingredients to a blender
2. Blend until you get a smooth and creamy texture
3. Serve chilled and enjoy!

Nutritional Contents:

- Calories: 312
- Fat: 25g
- Carbohydrates: 14g
- Protein: 9g

Brewed Green Tea Smoothie

Serving: 4

Prep Time: 10 minutes

Ingredients:

- 2 large avocados, pitted and peeled
- 4 cups spinach
- ½ cup fresh mint leaves
- 2 cups green tea, brewed and cooled
- 4 stalks celery, chopped
- 2 grapefruits, peeled and frozen
- 4 cups pineapple, chunked and frozen
- ¼ teaspoon ground cayenne pepper

Directions:

4. Add all the listed ingredients to a blender

5. Blend until you have a smooth and creamy texture

6. Serve chilled and enjoy!

Nutritional Contents:

- Calories: 155
- Fat: 0.4g
- Carbohydrates: 8g
- Protein: 5.6g

Chapter 3: Alkalizing Smoothies Protect Your Bones and Kidneys

Hearty Alkaline Strawberry Summer Deluxe

Serving: 2

Prep Time: 5 minutes

Ingredients:

- 2 cups of coconut water
- ½ cup strawberries or blueberries, organic
- Half banana
- ½ inch ginger
- Juice of 2 grapefruits

Directions:

1. Add listed ingredients to a blender
2. Blend until you have a smooth and creamy texture
3. Serve chilled and enjoy!

Nutritional Contents:

- Calories: 450
- Fat: 37g
- Carbohydrates: 20g
- Protein: 16g

Grapefruit, Pineapple, and Black Pepper Smoothie

Serving: 2

Prep Time: 5 minutes

Ingredients:

- 1 cup grapefruit, chopped
- ½ teaspoon black pepper, freshly ground
- 1 cup pineapple, ripe
- A pinch of Himalayan pink salt

Directions:

1. Add all the listed ingredients to a blender

2. Blend until you have a smooth and creamy texture

3. Serve chilled and enjoy!

Nutritional Contents:

- Calories: 121
- Fat: 1g
- Carbohydrates: 15g
- Protein: 3g

Spinach, Strawberry and Cinnamon Smoothie

Serving: 2

Prep Time: 5 minutes

Ingredients:

- 1 cup baby spinach
- ½ teaspoon Ceylon cinnamon powder
- ½ cup strawberries, chopped

Directions:

1. Add all the listed ingredients to a blender

2. Blend until you have a smooth and creamy texture

3. Serve chilled and enjoy!

Nutritional Contents:

- Calories: 114
- Fat: 1g
- Carbohydrates: 22g
- Protein: 5g

Mango Kiwi Smoothie

Serving: 2

Prep Time: 10 minutes

Ingredients:

- 2 kiwis, peeled
- 2 mangoes, peeled, pit removed and chopped
- 16 ice cubes
- 2 bananas
- 4 teaspoons honey

Directions:

1. Add all the listed ingredients to a blender
2. Blend until you have a smooth and creamy texture
3. Serve chilled and enjoy!

Nutritional Contents:

- Calories: 198
- Fat: 1g
- Carbohydrates: 0g
- Protein: 2.5g

Feisty Mango and Coconut Smoothie

Serving: 2

Prep Time: 5 minutes

Ingredients:

- 1 cup coconut milk, unsweetened
- ½ cup spinach
- 1 teaspoon spirulina
- 1 cup of frozen mango

Directions:

1. Dice the mangoes nicely
2. Add all the listed ingredients to a blender
3. Blend on medium until you have a smooth and creamy texture
4. Serve chilled and enjoy!

Nutritional Contents:

- Calories: 138
- Fat: 12g
- Carbohydrates: 8g
- Protein: 2g

Subtle Strawberry and Spinach Delight

Serving: 1

Prep Time: 10 minutes

Ingredients:

- ½ cup strawberries, chopped
- ½ cup whole milk yogurt
- 1 tablespoon MCT oil
- 1 tablespoon hemp seed
- 1 tablespoon flaxseed, ground
- 1 ½ cups of water
- 1 cup spinach
- 1 pack stevia

Directions:

1. Add listed ingredients to a blender

2. Blend until you get a smooth and creamy texture

3. Serve chilled and enjoy!

Nutritional Contents:

- Calories: 334
- Fat: 26g
- Carbohydrates: 14g
- Protein: 10g

Peach, Passion Fruit, and Flax Seeds Smoothie

Serving: 2

Prep Time: 5 minutes

Ingredients:

- 2 peaches, chopped
- 1 tablespoon flaxseeds, ground
- ½ cup of passion fruit
- A pinch of Himalayan pink salt

Directions:

1. Add all the listed ingredients to a blender
2. Blend until you have a smooth and creamy texture
3. Serve chilled and enjoy!

Nutritional Contents:

- Calories: 114
- Fat: 1g
- Carbohydrates: 22g
- Protein: 5g

Apple Pie Smoothie

Serving: 2

Prep Time: 10 minutes

Ingredients:

- 2 apples, cored and peeled
- ¼ teaspoon nutmeg
- ½ teaspoon cinnamon
- ½ cup blueberries
- 2 cups spinach, raw
- 2 cups of water
- 2 teaspoons vanilla extract

Directions:

1. Add listed ingredients to a blender
2. Blend until you have a smooth and creamy texture
3. Serve chilled and enjoy!

Nutritional Contents:

- Calories: 82
- Fat: 0.5g
- Carbohydrates: 19.4g
- Protein: 1g

Strawberry Lime Smoothie

Serving: 2

Prep Time: 5 minutes

Ingredients:

- 1 ½ ounces baby spinach
- 3 ounces strawberries
- 1 teaspoon baobab powder
- 1 tablespoon flaxseed
- 1 banana, peeled
- ½ lime, juiced
- 1 cup of coconut water
- 1 cup ice

Directions:

1. Add all the listed ingredients to a blender
2. Blend until you have a smooth and creamy texture
3. Serve chilled and enjoy!

Nutritional Contents:

- Calories: 130
- Fat: 2g
- Carbohydrates: 25g
- Protein: 3g

Creamy Berry Smoothie

Serving: 1

Prep Time: 10 minutes

Ingredients:

- ½ cup mixed berries(strawberries, blueberries, raspberries, blackberries)
- ½ teaspoon cinnamon
- 2 cups of coconut milk
- ½ cup heavy whipping cream

Directions:

1. Add all the listed ingredients to a blender

2. Blend until you have a smooth and creamy texture

3. Serve chilled and enjoy!

Nutritional Contents:

- Calories: 338
- Fat: 28.8g
- Carbohydrates: 9.4g
- Protein: 3.2g

Chapter 4: Anti-Aging Smoothies

The Super Green

Serving: 1

Prep Time: 10 minutes

Ingredients:

- 1 tablespoon agave nectar
- 1 bunch kale, spinach, Swiss chard or combination
- 1 bunch cilantro
- 2 cucumbers, chopped and peeled
- 1 lime, peeled
- 1 lemon, outer yellow peeled
- 1 orange, peeled
- ½ cup ice

Directions:

1. Add all the listed ingredients to a blender
2. Blend until you have a smooth and creamy texture
3. Serve chilled and enjoy!

Nutritional Contents:

- Calories: 3180
- Fat: 15g
- Carbohydrates: 8g
- Protein: 5g

The Wrinkle Fighter

Serving: 1

Prep Time: 10 minutes

Ingredients:

- 2 brazil nuts
- 1 tablespoon flaxseeds
- 1 orange, peeled and cut in half
- 2 cups wild blueberries, frozen
- 2 cups kale, roughly chopped
- 1 ½ cups cold coconut water

Directions:

1. Add all the listed ingredients to a blender
2. Blend until you have a smooth and creamy texture
3. Serve chilled and enjoy!

Nutritional Contents:

- Calories: 180
- Fat: 15g
- Carbohydrates: 8g
- Protein: 5g

The Anti-Aging Turmeric and Coconut Delight

Serving: 1

Prep Time: 10 minutes

Ingredients:

- 1 tablespoon coconut oil
- 2 teaspoons chia seeds
- 1 teaspoon ground turmeric
- 1 banana, frozen
- ½ cup pineapple, diced
- 1 cup of coconut milk

Directions:

1. Add all the listed ingredients to a blender

2. Blend until you have a smooth and creamy texture

3. Serve chilled and enjoy!

Nutritional Contents:

- Calories: 430
- Fat: 30g
- Carbohydrates: 10g
- Protein: 7g

The Anti-Aging Superfood Glass

Serving: 1

Prep Time: 10 minutes

Ingredients:

- Water as needed
- ½ cup unsweetened nut milk
- 1-2 scoops vanilla Whey Protein
- 1 tablespoon unrefined coconut oil
- 1 tablespoon chia seeds
- 1 tablespoon almond butter
- ¼ cup frozen blueberries
- ½ stick frozen acai puree

Directions:

1. Add all the listed ingredients to a blender

2. Blend until you have a smooth and creamy texture

3. Serve chilled and enjoy!

Nutritional Contents:

- Calories: 162
- Fat: 14g
- Carbohydrates: 10g
- Protein: 3g

The Glass of Glowing Skin

Serving: 1

Prep Time: 10 minutes

Ingredients:

- ½ avocado, sliced
- 2 cups kale
- 1 cup mango, chopped
- 1 cup pineapple, chopped
- 2 frozen bananas, peeled and sliced
- ½ cup of coconut water
- 1 tablespoon flax

Directions:

1. Add all the listed ingredients to a blender
2. Blend until you have a smooth and creamy texture
3. Serve chilled and enjoy!

Nutritional Contents:

- Calories: 430
- Fat: 40g
- Carbohydrates: 20g
- Protein: 10g

The Feisty Goddess

Serving: 1

Prep Time: 10 minutes

Ingredients:

- 1 cup unsweetened almond milk
- 2 tablespoons lemon juice
- 2 tablespoons avocado, peeled and pit removed
- 1 tablespoon sunflower seeds
- ½ medium banana, ripe
- 1 cup packed spinach

Directions:

1. Add all the listed ingredients to a blender

2. Blend until you have a smooth and creamy texture

3. Serve chilled and enjoy!

Nutritional Contents:

- Calories: 401
- Fat: 42g
- Carbohydrates: 4g
- Protein: 2g

The Breezy Blueberry

Serving: 1

Prep Time: 10 minutes

Ingredients:

- Handful of mint
- 1 teaspoon chia seeds
- 1 tablespoon lemon juice
- 1 cup of coconut water
- 1 cup strawberries
- 1 cup blueberries

Directions:

1. Add all the listed ingredients to a blender

2. Blend until you have a smooth and creamy texture

3. Serve chilled and enjoy!

Nutritional Contents:

- Calories: 169
- Fat: 13g
- Carbohydrates: 11g
- Protein: 6g

Powerful Kale and Carrot Glass

Serving: 1

Prep Time: 10 minutes

Ingredients:

- 1 cup of coconut water
- Lemon juice, 1 lemon
- 1 green apple, core removed and chopped
- 1 carrot, chopped
- 1 cup kale

Directions:

1. Add all the listed ingredients to a blender
2. Blend until you have a smooth and creamy texture
3. Serve chilled and enjoy!

Nutritional Contents:

- Calories: 116
- Fat: 5g
- Carbohydrates: 14g
- Protein: 6g

A Tropical Glass of Chia

Serving: 1

Prep Time: 10 minutes

Ingredients:

- 1 cup coconut water
- 1 tablespoon chia seeds
- 1 cup pineapple, sliced
- ½ cup mango, sliced

Directions:

1. Add all the listed ingredients to a blender

2. Blend until you have a smooth and creamy texture

3. Serve chilled and enjoy!

Nutritional Contents:

- Calories: 90
- Fat: 5g
- Carbohydrates: 11g
- Protein: 4g

Simple Anti-Aging Cacao Dream

Serving: 1

Prep Time: 10 minutes

Ingredients:

- 1 cup unsweetened almond milk
- 1 tablespoon cacao powder
- 6 strawberries
- 1 banana

Directions:

1. Add all the listed ingredients to a blender

2. Blend until you have a smooth and creamy texture

3. Serve chilled and enjoy!

Nutritional Contents:

- Calories: 220
- Fat: 9g
- Carbohydrates: 20g
- Protein: 6g

Chapter 5: Antioxidant Smoothies

The Gut Heavy Smoothie

Serving: 1

Prep Time: 10 minutes

Ingredients:

- 2-3 cups spinach leaves
- ½ cup frozen blueberries, unsweetened
- 1 serving aloe vera leaves
- ½ cup plain full-fat yogurt
- 1 scoop Pinnaclife prebiotic fiber
- 1 and ½ tablespoons coconut oil, unrefined
- 1 tablespoon chia seeds
- 1 tablespoon hemp hearts
- 1 cup of water

Directions:

1. Add listed ingredients to a blender
2. Blend until you have a smooth and creamy texture
3. Serve chilled and enjoy!

Nutritional Contents:

- Calories: 409
- Fat: 33g
- Carbohydrates: 8g
- Protein: 12g

Fresh Purple Fig Smoothie

Serving: 2

Prep Time: 5 minutes

Ingredients:

- 1 fig
- 1 cup grapes
- ½ teaspoon maqui powder
- 1 cup of water
- 1 pear, chopped

Directions:

4. Add all the listed ingredients to a blender
5. Blend until you have a smooth and creamy texture
6. Serve chilled and enjoy!

Nutritional Contents:

- Calories: 136
- Fat: 4g
- Carbohydrates: 28g
- Protein: 3g

Mesmerizing Strawberry and Chocolate Shake

Serving: 1

Prep Time: 10 minutes

Ingredients:

- ½ cup strawberry, sliced
- 1 tablespoons coconut flake, unsweetened
- 1 and ½ cups of water
- ½ cup heavy cream, liquid
- 1 tablespoon cocoa powder
- 1 pack stevia

Directions:

1. Add all the listed ingredients to a blender

2. Blend on medium until you have a smooth

3. Serve chilled and enjoy!

Nutritional Contents:

- Calories: 470
- Fat: 46g
- Carbohydrates: 15g
- Protein: 4g

The Strawberry Almond Smoothie

Serving: 1

Prep Time: 10 minutes

Ingredients:

- ¼ cup frozen strawberries, unsweetened
- 16 ounces unsweetened almond milk, vanilla
- 1 scoop vanilla whey protein
- 1 pack stevia
- 4 ounces heavy cream

Directions:

1. Add all the listed ingredients into your blender

2. Blend until smooth

3. Serve chilled and enjoy!

Nutritional Contents:

- Calories: 304
- Fat: 25g
- Carbohydrates: 7g
- Protein: 15g

Hazelnut and Coconut Medley

Serving: 1

Prep Time: 10 minutes

Ingredients:

- ¼ cup hazelnuts, chopped
- ½ cup of coconut milk
- 1 pack stevia
- 1 and ½ cups of water

Directions:

1. Add all the listed ingredients into your blender
2. Blend until smooth
3. Serve chilled and enjoy!

Nutritional Contents:

- Calories: 457
- Fat: 46g
- Carbohydrates: 12g
- Protein: 7g

Overloaded Hazelnut and Mocha Shake

Serving: 1

Prep Time: 10 minutes

Ingredients:

- 1-ounce Hazelnuts
- 2 cups brewed coffee, chilled
- 1 tablespoon MCT oil
- 2 tablespoons cocoa powder
- 1-2 packet Stevia, optional

Directions:

1. Add all the listed ingredients into your blender

2. Blend until smooth

3. Serve chilled and enjoy!

Nutritional Contents:

- Calories: 325
- Fat: 33g
- Carbohydrates: 12g
- Protein: 6.8g

The Nutty Smoothie

Serving: 1

Prep Time: 10 minutes

Ingredients:

- 1-ounce Hazelnut
- 1 ounce Macadamia Nuts
- 1 tablespoon chia seeds
- 1-2 packets Stevia, optional
- 2 cups of water

Directions:

4. Add all the listed ingredients to a blender
5. Blend on high until smooth and creamy
6. Enjoy your smoothie!

Nutritional Contents:

- Calories: 452
- Fat: 43g
- Carbohydrates: 15g
- Protein: 9g

The Feisty Nut Shake

Serving: 1

Prep Time: 10 minutes

Ingredients:

- ¼ cup almonds, sliced
- ¼ cup macadamia nuts, whole
- 1 tablespoon flaxseed
- ¼ cup heavy cream, liquid
- ½ tablespoon cocoa powder
- 1 cup of water
- 1 tablespoon hemp seed
- 1 pack stevia

Directions:

1. Add listed ingredients to a blender
2. Blend until you have a smooth and creamy texture
3. Serve chilled and enjoy!

Nutritional Contents:

- Calories: 590
- Fat: 57g
- Carbohydrates: 17g
- Protein: 12g

The Dashing Coconut and Melon

Serving: 1

Prep Time: 10 minutes

Ingredients:

- ½ cup melon, sliced
- 1 tablespoon coconut flakes, unsweetened
- ¼ cup whole milk yogurt
- 1 tablespoon coconut oil
- 1 tablespoon chia seeds
- 1 pack stevia
- 1 and ½ cups of water

Directions:

1. Add listed ingredients to a blender

2. Blend until you have a smooth and creamy texture

3. Serve chilled and enjoy!

Nutritional Contents:

- Calories: 278
- Fat: 21g
- Carbohydrates: 15g
- Protein: 6g

Cayenne Spices Chocolate Shake

Serving: 1

Prep Time: 10 minutes

Ingredients:

- ½ pinch cayenne powder
- 2 tablespoons coconut oil, unrefined
- ¼ cup coconut cream
- 1 tablespoon chia seeds, whole
- 2 tablespoons cacao
- Dash of vanilla extract
- ½-1 cup water
- Ice cubes

Directions:

1. Add listed ingredients to a blender

2. Blend until you have a smooth and creamy texture

3. Serve chilled and enjoy!

Nutritional Contents:

- Calories: 258
- Fat: 26g
- Carbohydrates: 3g
- Protein: 3g

Chapter 6: Cleansing Smoothies
Apple Celery Detox Smoothie

Serving: 2

Prep Time: 10 minutes

Ingredients:

- 3 tablespoons collard greens
- 2 ribs celery
- 3 springs mint
- 1 apple, chopped
- 2 tablespoons hazelnuts, raw
- ½ teaspoon moringa
- 1 cup of water
- 1 cup ice

Directions:

1. Add all the listed ingredients to a blender
2. Blend until you have a smooth and creamy texture
3. Serve chilled and enjoy!

Nutritional Contents:

- Calories: 115
- Fat: 5g
- Carbohydrates: 14g
- Protein: 3g

Zucchini Detox Smoothie

Serving: 2

Prep Time: 10 minutes

Ingredients:

- 1 zucchini
- 1 tablespoon sea beans
- ½ lemon, juiced
- 1 teaspoon maqui berry powder
- 8 tablespoons grape tomatoes
- 6 tablespoons celery stocks
- ½ jalapeno pepper, seeded
- 1 cup of water
- 1 cup ice

Directions:

1. Add all the listed ingredients to blender except zucchini

2. Add zucchini and blend the mixture

3. Blend until smooth

4. Serve chilled and enjoy!

Nutritional Contents:

- Calories: 50
- Fat: 0.5g
- Carbohydrates: 10g
- Protein: 2.4g

Carrot Detox Smoothie

Serving: 2

Prep Time: 10 minutes

Ingredients:

- 10 tablespoons carrot, chopped
- 1-inch ginger, peeled and chopped
- 1 teaspoon cinnamon
- 1 banana, peeled
- 1-inch turmeric peeled, chopped
- 1 cup of coconut milk
- 1 cup ice

Directions:

1. Add all the listed ingredients to a blender
2. Blend until smooth
3. Serve chilled and enjoy!

Nutritional Contents:

- Calories: 134
- Fat: 3g
- Carbohydrates: 30g
- Protein: 2g

Pear Jicama Detox Smoothie

Serving: 2

Prep Time: 10 minutes

Ingredients:

- 3 tablespoons red kale
- 8 tablespoons jicama, peeled and chopped
- 1 lemon, juiced
- 1 pear, chopped
- 1 teaspoon reishi mushroom
- 1 tablespoon flaxseed
- 1 cup of water
- 1 cup ice

Directions:

1. Add all the listed ingredients to a blender

2. Blend until smooth

3. Serve chilled and enjoy!

Nutritional Contents:

- Calories: 102
- Fat: 0g
- Carbohydrates: 24g
- Protein: 2g

Coconut Pineapple Detox Smoothie

Serving: 2

Prep Time: 10 minutes

Ingredients:

- 3 tablespoons Swiss Chard
- 2 tablespoons coconut flakes
- 1 tablespoon chia seeds
- 8 tablespoons pineapple, peeled and chopped
- ½ avocado pitted
- 1 orange, peeled
- 1 cup of water
- 1 cup ice

Directions:

1. Add all the listed ingredients to a blender
2. Blend until smooth
3. Serve chilled and enjoy!

Nutritional Contents:

- Calories: 212
- Fat: 0g
- Carbohydrates: 26g
- Protein: 3g

Pineapple Coconut Detox Smoothie

Serving: 2

Prep Time: 10 minutes

Ingredients:

- 4 cups kale, chopped
- 2 cups of coconut water
- 2 bananas
- 2 cups pineapple

Directions:

1. Add all the listed ingredients to a blender

2. Blend until you have a smooth and creamy texture

3. Serve chilled and enjoy!

Nutritional Contents:

- Calories: 299
- Fat: 1.1g
- Carbohydrates: 71.5g
- Protein: 7.9g

Avocado Detox Smoothie

Serving: 3

Prep Time: 10 minutes

Ingredients:

- 4 cups spinach, chopped
- 1 avocado, chopped
- 3 cups apple juice
- 2 apples, unpeeled, cored and chopped

Directions:

1. Add all the listed ingredients to a blender

2. Blend until you have a smooth and creamy texture

3. Serve chilled and enjoy!

Nutritional Contents:

- Calories: 336
- Fat: 13.8g
- Carbohydrates: 55.8g
- Protein: 3g

Chamomile Ginger Detox Smoothie

Serving: 2

Prep Time: 10 minutes

Ingredients:

- 3 tablespoons collard greens
- 1 tablespoon chamomile flowers, dried
- 1 pear, chopped
- 1 cantaloupe, sliced and chopped
- ½ inch ginger, peeled
- ½ lemon, juiced
- 1 cup ice
- 1 cup of water

Directions:

1. Add all the listed ingredients to a blender

2. Blend until smooth

3. Serve chilled and enjoy!

Nutritional Contents:

- Calories: 86
- Fat: 0g
- Carbohydrates: 22g
- Protein: 2g

Wheatgrass Detox Smoothie

Serving: 2

Prep Time: 10 minutes

Ingredients:

- 3 tablespoons Swiss chard
- 1 banana, peeled
- 3 tablespoons almonds
- 1 teaspoon wheatgrass powder
- 2 kiwis, peeled
- 1 cup ice
- 1 cup of water

Directions:

1. Add all the listed ingredients to blender except kiwis
2. Blend until smooth
3. Add kiwis and blend again
4. Serve chilled and enjoy!

Nutritional Contents:

- Calories: 154
- Fat: 6g
- Carbohydrates: 24g
- Protein: 4g

Charcoal Lemonade Detox Smoothie

Serving: 2

Prep Time: 10 minutes

Ingredients:

- 3 tablespoons collard green
- ½ teaspoon charcoal activated
- 1 apple, chopped
- 1 lemon, peeled
- ½ inch ginger
- 1 cucumber, chopped
- 1 cup ice
- 1 cup of water

Directions:

1. Add all the listed ingredients to blender except kiwis

2. Blend until smooth

3. Add kiwis and blend again

4. Serve chilled and enjoy!

Nutritional Contents:

- Calories: 88
- Fat: 0.6g
- Carbohydrates: 23g
- Protein: 2g

Chapter 7: Diabetic Smoothies

Choco Spinach Delight

Serving: 1

Prep Time: 10 minutes

Ingredients:

- 4 ice cubes
- 1 scoop green superfood
- 1 scoop protein powder
- 1 tablespoon chia seeds
- ½ cup berry yogurt
- 1 handful of organic spinach
- 1 teaspoon organic flaxseed
- ½ avocado
- 1/3 cup organic strawberries, frozen
- ½ cup organic blueberries, frozen
- ¾ cup unsweetened almond milk

Directions:

1. Add all the listed ingredients to a blender

2. Blend until you have a smooth and creamy texture

3. Serve chilled and enjoy!

Nutritional Contents:

- Calories: 180
- Fat: 16g
- Carbohydrates: 7g
- Protein: 1g

Diabetic Berry Blast

Serving: 1

Prep Time: 10 minutes

Ingredients:

- 2 tablespoons flax meal
- 3 kale leaves
- 2 cups unsweetened mango chunks
- 1 cup frozen raspberries
- 1 cup frozen blackberries
- 1 cup frozen blueberries

Directions:

1. Add all the listed ingredients to a blender

2. Blend until you have a smooth and creamy texture

3. Serve chilled and enjoy!

Nutritional Contents:

- Calories: 153
- Fat: 11g
- Carbohydrates: 8g
- Protein: 7g

The Great Dia Green Smoothie

Serving: 1

Prep Time: 10 minutes

Ingredients:

- 1 whole banana
- 1 cup kale
- 1 cup spinach
- 2 tablespoons chia seeds, soaked
- A handful of mixed berries

Directions:

1. Add all the listed ingredients to a blender

2. Blend until you have a smooth and creamy texture

3. Serve chilled and enjoy!

Nutritional Contents:

- Calories: 180
- Fat: 15g
- Carbohydrates: 8g
- Protein: 5g

Low Carb Berry Smoothie

Serving: 1

Prep Time: 10 minutes

Ingredients:

- 5 medium strawberry
- 6 ice cubes
- ½ cup low-fat Greek-style yogurt
- 1 cup unsweetened almond milk

Directions:

1. Add all the listed ingredients to a blender

2. Blend until you have a smooth and creamy texture

3. Serve chilled and enjoy!

Nutritional Contents:

- Calories: 167
- Fat: 6g
- Carbohydrates: 11g
- Protein: 16g

Avocado Turmeric Smoothie

Serving: 1

Prep Time: 10 minutes

Ingredients:

- 1 avocado
- 2 teaspoons lemon juice
- 1 teaspoon turmeric
- 2 teaspoons ginger, fresh grated
- 1 and ¼ cups of coconut milk
- 2 cups ice, crushed
- Stevia, to taste

Directions:

4. Add all the listed ingredients to a blender
5. Blend until you have a smooth and creamy texture
6. Serve chilled and enjoy!

Nutritional Contents:

- Calories: 320
- Fat: 27.4g
- Carbohydrates: 11g
- Protein: 4.3g

Pineapple Broccoli Smoothie

Serving: 2

Prep Time: 10 minutes

Ingredients:

- 1 cup strawberries
- 2 cups almond milk
- 2 cups broccoli florets
- ½ cup pineapple
- 2 teaspoons honey

Directions:

1. Add listed ingredients to a blender
2. Blend until you have a smooth and creamy texture
3. Serve chilled and enjoy!

Nutritional Contents:

- Calories: 324
- Fat: 25.4g
- Carbohydrates: 18g
- Protein: 4.3g

Chai Pumpkin Smoothie

Serving: 1

Prep Time: 10 minutes

Ingredients:

- 6 tablespoons pumpkin puree
- 2 teaspoons vanilla
- 1 teaspoon pumpkin pie spice
- 2 tablespoons vanilla
- 1 avocado, fresh
- 2 teaspoons loose chai tea, brewed
- 2 tablespoons MCT oil, optional

Directions:

4. Add all the listed ingredients to a blender
5. Blend until you have a smooth and creamy texture
6. Serve chilled and enjoy!

Nutritional Contents:

- Calories: 371
- Fat: 21.4g
- Carbohydrates: 10.3g
- Protein: 3.3g

Keto Mocha Smoothie

Serving: 4

Prep Time: 10 minutes

Ingredients:

- 6 tablespoons cocoa powder, unsweetened
- 1 cup of coconut milk
- 3 cups almond milk, unsweetened
- 2 avocados, cut in half
- 2 teaspoons vanilla extract
- 6 tablespoons erythritol, granulated
- 4 teaspoons instant coffee crystals

Directions:

1. Add all the listed ingredients to a blender
2. Blend until you have a smooth and creamy texture
3. Serve chilled and enjoy!

Nutritional Contents:

- Calories: 273
- Fat: 24.3g
- Carbohydrates: 8.2g
- Protein: 4.5g

Berry Truffle Smoothie

Serving: 2

Prep Time: 10 minutes

Ingredients:

- 1 medium Haas avocado
- 1 and ¼ teaspoons pure vanilla extract
- ½ cup whipping cream
- 3 tablespoons cocoa powder, unsweetened
- 4 tablespoons pecans
- 1 and ¼ cups mixed berries, frozen
- 2 pinches salt
- ¾ cups of ice cubes
- Erythritol, to taste
- 1 cup of water

Directions:

1. Add all the listed ingredients to a blender

2. Blend until you have a smooth and creamy texture

3. Serve chilled and enjoy!

Nutritional Contents:

- Calories: 375
- Fat: 32.5g
- Carbohydrates: 11.3g
- Protein: 5.8g

Chapter 8: Digestive Smoothies

Blueberry Chia Smoothie

Serving: 2

Prep Time: 10 minutes

Ingredients:

- 2 cups blueberries, frozen
- 1 cup coconut cream
- 4 tablespoons coconut oil
- 4 tablespoons swerve sweetener
- 4 tablespoons chia seeds, ground
- 2 cups full-fat Greek yogurt
- 2 cups almond milk, unsweetened

Directions:

4. Add all the listed ingredients to a blender
5. Blend until you have a smooth and creamy texture
6. Serve chilled and enjoy!

Nutritional Contents:

- Calories: 351
- Fat: 36g
- Carbohydrates: 12.8g
- Protein: 12.9g

Raspberry Chia Smoothie

Serving: 1

Prep Time: 10 minutes

Ingredients:

- 1 cup plain Greek yogurt, nonfat
- 1 cup raspberries
- 1 banana
- 2 mangoes, peeled, pit removed and chopped
- 1 teaspoon chia seeds

Directions:

1. Add all the listed ingredients to a blender

2. Blend until you have a smooth and creamy texture

3. Serve chilled and enjoy!

Nutritional Contents:

- Calories: 363
- Fat: 2.6g
- Carbohydrates: 82.3g
- Protein: 10.6g

Pineapple Yogurt Smoothie

Serving: 1

Prep Time: 10 minutes

Ingredients:

- 1 cup plain Greek yogurt, nonfat
- 1 cup apple juice, unsweetened
- 2 cups pineapple chunks
- 2 mangoes, peeled, pit removed and chopped
- 1 teaspoon chia seeds
- 16 ice cubes

Directions:

1. Add all the listed ingredients to a blender

2. Blend until you have a smooth and creamy texture

3. Serve chilled and enjoy!

Nutritional Contents:

- Calories: 382
- Fat: 1.6g
- Carbohydrates: 88.5g
- Protein: 11.2g

Chia-Berry Belly Blaster

Serving: 2

Prep Time: 5 minutes

Ingredients:

- 1 cup berries, frozen
- 1 cup plain Greek yogurt, unsweetened
- 1 tablespoon chia seeds, ground
- 1 tablespoon vanilla extract
- ½ cup ice

Directions:

1. Add all the listed ingredients to a blender

2. Blend until you have a smooth and creamy texture

3. Serve chilled and enjoy!

Nutritional Contents:

- Calories: 148
- Fat: 5g
- Carbohydrates: 26g
- Protein: 4g

Sapodilla, Chia and Almond Milk Smoothie

Serving: 2

Prep Time: 5 minutes

Ingredients:

- 4 medium sapodillas
- 2/3 cup almond milk
- 3 tablespoons chia seeds
- 1 tablespoon flakes

Directions:

1. Wash the sapodillas, peel them and then roughly chop them
2. Toss the chopped sapodillas into your blender
3. Then add almond milk
4. Add all the listed ingredients to a blender
5. Blend well and add almond on top
6. Serve and enjoy!

Nutritional Contents:

- Calories: 113
- Fat: 1g
- Carbohydrates: 21g
- Protein: 5g

Blueberry, Oats and Chia Smoothie

Serving: 2

Prep Time: 5 minutes

Ingredients:

- ½ cup blueberries
- 2 tablespoons chia seeds
- ¼ cup oats
- 2 cups low-fat milk

Directions:

4. Add all the listed ingredients to a blender
5. Blend until you have a smooth and creamy texture
6. Serve chilled and enjoy!

Nutritional Contents:

- Calories: 140
- Fat: 3g
- Carbohydrates: 25g
- Protein: 6g

Apple Chia Detox Smoothie

Serving: 2

Prep Time: 5 minutes

Ingredients:

- 3 tablespoons collard greens
- 1 mini cucumber
- 1 tablespoon chia seeds
- 4 kumquats
- 1 apple, chopped
- ½ teaspoon chia seeds
- 1 cup ice
- 1 cup of water

Directions:

1. Add all the listed ingredients to a blender

2. Blend until you have a smooth and creamy texture

3. Serve chilled and enjoy!

Nutritional Contents:

- Calories: 108
- Fat: 2g
- Carbohydrates: 21g
- Protein: 3g

Banana Oatmeal Detox Smoothie

Serving: 2

Prep Time: 10 minutes

Ingredients:

- 3 tablespoons collard greens
- 3 tablespoons oats
- 1 banana, peeled
- 1 apple, chopped
- 1 teaspoon cinnamon
- 1 cup ice
- 1 cup of water

Directions:

1. Add all the listed ingredients to a blender
2. Blend until you have a smooth and creamy texture
3. Serve chilled and enjoy!

Nutritional Contents:

- Calories: 162
- Fat: 1g
- Carbohydrates: 41g
- Protein: 3g

The Nutty Macadamia Delight

Serving: 1

Prep Time: 10 minutes

Ingredients:

- Oz Macadamia nuts
- 1 cup spinach
- 1 tablespoon chia seeds
- 1 packet stevia, if you want
- 2/3 cup water
- ¼ cup heavy cream

Directions:

1. Add all the listed ingredients into your blender

2. Blend until smooth

3. Serve chilled and enjoy!

Nutritional Contents:

- Calories: 485
- Fat: 48g
- Carbohydrates: 13g
- Protein: 7g

Basic Green Banana Smoothie

Serving: 1

Prep Time: 5 minutes

Ingredients:

- 1 cup blueberries, frozen
- 1 cup almond milk
- 1 cup banana, frozen
- 1 cup spinach
- ½ tablespoon chia seeds

Directions:

1. Add all the listed ingredients to blender except kiwis
2. Blend until smooth
3. Add kiwis and blend again
4. Serve chilled and enjoy!

Nutritional Contents:

- Calories: 146
- Fat: 3g
- Carbohydrates: 30g
- Protein: 3g

Chapter 9: High-Energy Smoothies

Pumpkin Power Smoothie

Serving: 2

Prep Time: 10 minutes

Ingredients:

- 2 cups pumpkin puree
- 2 pumpkin pie spice, dashes
- 1 banana, frozen
- 2 dashes pie spice, dashes
- 2 handfuls ice cubes

Directions:

1. Add all the listed ingredients to a blender
2. Blend until you have a smooth and creamy texture
3. Serve chilled and enjoy!

Nutritional Contents:

- Calories: 177
- Fat: 3.9g
- Carbohydrates: 35.3g
- Protein: 4.4g

Peppermint Stick Smoothie

Serving: 2

Prep Time: 5 minutes

Ingredients:

- 1 banana, peeled
- 1 tablespoon coconut milk
- 4 spring mint
- 1 and ½ tablespoons cacao powder
- 1 apple, chopped
- 1 cup ice
- 1 cup of water

Directions:

1. Add all the listed ingredients to a blender
2. Blend until you have a smooth and creamy texture
3. Serve chilled and enjoy!

Nutritional Contents:

- Calories: 150
- Fat: 5g
- Carbohydrates: 29g
- Protein: 2g

Persimmon Pineapple Protein Smoothie

Serving: 2

Prep Time: 5 minutes

Ingredients:

- 1 persimmon, topped and chopped
- 1 tablespoon cinnamon
- 1 squash
- 1 tablespoon flaxseed
- 4 ounces pineapple
- 1 tablespoon pea protein
- 1 cup of water

Directions:

1. Add all the listed ingredients to a blender

2. Blend until you have a smooth and creamy texture

3. Serve chilled and enjoy!

Nutritional Contents:

- Calories: 159
- Fat: 2g
- Carbohydrates: 33g
- Protein: 7g

MCT Strawberry Smoothie

Serving: 2

Prep Time: 10 minutes

Ingredients:

- 1 and ¼ cups of coconut milk
- 4 tablespoons strawberry
- ½ cup heavy whipping cream
- 14 large ice cubes
- ½ teaspoon xanthan gum
- 2 tablespoons MCT oil

Directions:

1. Add all the listed ingredients to a blender

2. Blend until you have a smooth and creamy texture

3. Serve chilled and enjoy!

Nutritional Contents:

- Calories: 373
- Fat: 45.1g
- Carbohydrates: 5.8g
- Protein: 2.1g

Mango Citrus Smoothie

Serving: 1

Prep Time: 10 minutes

Ingredients:

- 2 mangoes, peeled, pit removed and chopped
- 2 bananas
- 2 cups Greek yogurt, nonfat
- 2 cups orange juice
- 10 ice cubes

Directions:

1. Add all the listed ingredients to a blender
2. Blend until you have a smooth and creamy texture
3. Serve chilled and enjoy!

Nutritional Contents:

- Calories: 379
- Fat: 6.8g
- Carbohydrates: 76.3g
- Protein: 9.1g

Cinnamon Mango Smoothie

Serving: 2

Prep Time: 10 minutes

Ingredients:

- 2 mangoes, peeled, pit removed and chopped
- ½ teaspoon cinnamon, grounded
- 2 teaspoons lime juice
- 2 cups plain yogurt, low-fat
- 1 tablespoon honey

Directions:

1. Add all the listed ingredients to a blender
2. Blend until you have a smooth and creamy texture
3. Serve chilled and enjoy!

Nutritional Contents:

- Calories: 210
- Fat: 2.2g
- Carbohydrates: 40.2g
- Protein: 8.5g

Mango Honey Smoothie

Serving: 2

Prep Time: 10 minutes

Ingredients:

- 2 mangoes, peeled, pit removed and chopped
- 4 teaspoons honey
- 3 cups almond milk
- 16 ice cubes

Directions:

4. Add all the listed ingredients to a blender
5. Blend until you have a smooth and creamy texture
6. Serve chilled and enjoy!

Nutritional Contents:

- Calories: 223
- Fat: 3.4g
- Carbohydrates: 49.2g
- Protein: 2.9g

Orange Antioxidant Refresher

Serving: 2

Prep Time: 5 minutes

Ingredients:

- 4 ounces pineapple
- 1 orange, peeled
- 1 teaspoon pomegranate powder
- 1 mini orange, peeled
- ½ teaspoon turmeric
- ½ teaspoon ginger
- 1 cup ice
- 1 cup of water

Directions:

1. Add all the listed ingredients to a blender

2. Blend until you have a smooth and creamy texture

3. Serve chilled and enjoy!

Nutritional Contents:

- Calories: 101
- Fat: 1g
- Carbohydrates: 25g
- Protein: 2g

Zesty Orange Smoothie

Serving: 2

Prep Time: 10 minutes

Ingredients:

- 3 tablespoons baby spinach
- 1 apple, chopped
- 1 lime, peeled
- 1 cucumber, chopped
- 1 orange, peeled
- 1 tablespoon flaxseed
- 1 cup of water
- 1 cup ice

Directions:

4. Add all the listed ingredients to a blender
5. Blend until smooth
6. Serve chilled and enjoy!

Nutritional Contents:

- Calories: 112
- Fat: 2g
- Carbohydrates: 27g
- Protein: 2g

Berry Flax Smoothie

Serving: 4

Prep Time: 10 minutes

Ingredients:

- 3 cups dairy-free milk
- 2 cups spinach
- 2 tablespoons flaxseeds, ground
- 1 cup berries, fresh or frozen
- 2 teaspoons ginger root, peeled

Directions:

1. Add all the listed ingredients to a blender
2. Blend until you have a smooth and creamy texture
3. Serve chilled and enjoy!

Nutritional Contents:

- Calories: 212
- Fat: 11.9g
- Carbohydrates: 31.7g
- Protein: 7.3g

Chapter 10: Green Smoothies Recipes

The Curious Raspberry and Green Shake

Serving: 1

Prep Time: 10 minutes

Ingredients:

- ¼ cup raspberry
- 1 tablespoon macadamia oil
- 1 cup whole milk
- 1 pack stevia
- 1 cup spinach
- 1 cup of water

Directions:

1. Add listed ingredients to a blender

2. Blend until you get a smooth and creamy texture

3. Serve chilled and enjoy!

Nutritional Contents:

- Calories: 292
- Fat: 21g
- Carbohydrates: 17g
- Protein: 9g

The Green Minty Smoothie

Serving: 1

Prep Time: 10 minutes

Ingredients:

- 2 ounces almonds
- 1 cup spinach
- 2 mint leaves
- 1 stalk celery
- 2 cups of water
- 1 packet Stevia

Directions:

1. Add all the listed ingredients into your blender

2. Blend until smooth

3. Serve chilled and enjoy!

Nutritional Contents:

- Calories: 417
- Fat: 43g
- Carbohydrates: 10g
- Protein: 5.5g

A Mean Green Milk Shake

Serving: 1

Prep Time: 10 minutes

Ingredients:

- 1 cup whole milk
- 1 tablespoon coconut flakes, unsweetened
- 1 cup of water
- 2 cups spring mix salad
- 1 tablespoon coconut oil
- 1 pack stevia

Directions:

1. Add listed ingredients to a blender
2. Blend until you have a smooth and creamy texture
3. Serve chilled and enjoy!

Nutritional Contents:

- Calories: 309
- Fat: 23g
- Carbohydrates: 18g
- Protein: 9.5g

Garden Variety Green and Yogurt Delight

Serving: 1

Prep Time: 10 minutes

Ingredients:

- 1 cup whole milk yogurt
- 1 tablespoon flaxseed, ground
- 1 cup garden greens
- 1 tablespoon MCT oil
- 1 cup of water
- 1 pack stevia

Directions:

1. Add listed ingredients to a blender

2. Blend until you have a smooth and creamy texture

3. Serve chilled and enjoy!

Nutritional Contents:

- Calories: 334
- Fat: 26g
- Carbohydrates: 14g
- Protein: 11g

The Coolest 5 Lettuce Green Shake

Serving: 1

Prep Time: 10 minutes

Ingredients:

- 1 tablespoon MCT oil
- 1 tablespoon chia seeds
- 2 cups 5 – lettuce mix salad greens
- ¾ cup whole milk yogurt
- 1 pack stevia
- 1 ½ cups of water

Directions:

1. Add listed ingredients to a blender

2. Blend until you have a smooth and creamy texture

3. Serve chilled and enjoy!

Nutritional Contents:

- Calories: 320
- Fat: 24g
- Carbohydrates: 17g
- Protein: 10g

Passion Green Smoothie

Serving: 2

Prep Time: 10 minutes

Ingredients:

- 1 cup strawberries
- 2 cups spinach, raw
- ½ cup blueberries
- ½ cup Greek yogurt
- 2 cups of water

Directions:

1. Add listed ingredients to a blender
2. Blend until you have a smooth and creamy texture
3. Serve chilled and enjoy!

Nutritional Contents:

- Calories: 88
- Fat: 1.5g
- Carbohydrates: 13.9g
- Protein: 6.6g

Banana Green Smoothie

Serving: 2

Prep Time: 10 minutes

Ingredients:

- 2 bananas
- 1 cup strawberries
- 1 cup almond milk
- 2 cups spinach, raw
- 2 teaspoons vanilla extract

Directions:

1. Add listed ingredients to a blender
2. Blend until you have a smooth and creamy texture
3. Serve chilled and enjoy!

Nutritional Contents:

- Calories: 212
- Fat: 14.7g
- Carbohydrates: 20.4g
- Protein: 2.7g

Citrus Green Smoothie

Serving: 2

Prep Time: 10 minutes

Ingredients:

- 2 oranges, peeled
- 2 cups almond milk
- 1 cup strawberries
- 2 cups spinach, raw

Directions:

1. Add listed ingredients to a blender
2. Blend until you have a smooth and creamy texture
3. Serve chilled and enjoy!

Nutritional Contents:

- Calories: 334
- Fat: 28.9g
- Carbohydrates: 20.8g
- Protein: 4.3g

Electrifying Green Smoothie

Serving: 2

Prep Time: 10 minutes

Ingredients:

- ½ cup pineapple, peeled and chopped
- 2 cups almond milk
- 2 oranges, peeled
- 2 cups spinach, raw

Directions:

1. Slice the peeled oranges, then remove the seeds
2. Add listed ingredients to a blender
3. Blend until you have a smooth and creamy texture
4. Serve chilled and enjoy!

Nutritional Contents:

- Calories: 209
- Fat: 6.4g
- Carbohydrates: 38.4g
- Protein: 4.8g

Glowing Green Smoothie

Serving: 2

Prep Time: 10 minutes

Ingredients:

- 2 bananas
- 2 kiwis
- 4 celery stalks
- ½ cup pineapple
- 2 cups of water
- 4 cups spinach

Directions:

1. Add all the listed ingredients to a blender

2. Blend until you have a smooth and creamy texture

3. Serve chilled and enjoy!

Nutritional Contents:

- Calories: 191
- Fat: 1.1g
- Carbohydrates: 46.5g
- Protein: 7.8g

Chapter 11: Healthy Skin Smoothies

Mango Cucumber Smoothie

Serving: 2

Prep Time: 10 minutes

Ingredients:

- ½ cup mango
- 2 cups cucumber, chopped
- 2 oranges, peeled
- 2 tablespoons flaxseeds
- 2 cups spinach

Directions:

1. Add all the listed ingredients to a blender
2. Blend until you have a smooth and creamy texture
3. Serve chilled and enjoy!

Nutritional Contents:

- Calories: 146
- Fat: 2.8g
- Carbohydrates: 28.4g
- Protein: 4.4g

Pineapple Date Smoothie

Serving: 1

Prep Time: 10 minutes

Ingredients:

- 2 cups pineapple, chopped
- ¼ cup lemon juice
- 2 English cucumber
- 24 dates, pitted
- 3 cups of water

Directions:

1. Add all the listed ingredients to a blender
2. Blend until you have a smooth and creamy texture
3. Serve chilled and enjoy!

Nutritional Contents:

- Calories: 208
- Fat: 0.6g
- Carbohydrates: 54g
- Protein: 7.6g

Ginger Detox Smoothie

Serving: 2

Prep Time: 5 minutes

Ingredients:

- 1 apple, chopped
- 2 Persian cucumbers, chopped
- 1 Meyer lemon, peeled
- ½ teaspoon chlorella
- ½ inch ginger
- 1 ½ ounces collard green
- 1 cup of water

Directions:

1. Add all the listed ingredients to a blender
2. Blend until you have a smooth and creamy texture
3. Serve chilled and enjoy!

Nutritional Contents:

- Calories: 114
- Fat: 1g
- Carbohydrates: 22g
- Protein: 5g

Magical Blueberry and Kale Mix

Serving: 1

Prep Time: 10 minutes

Ingredients:

- ¼ cup blueberries
- 1 cup baby kale greens
- ½ cup whole milk yogurt
- 1 tablespoon MCT oil
- 1 tablespoon pepitas
- 1 tablespoon flaxseed, ground
- 1 ½ cups of water
- 1 pack stevia

Directions:

1. Add listed ingredients to a blender
2. Blend until you have a smooth and creamy texture
3. Serve chilled and enjoy!

Nutritional Contents:

- Calories: 307
- Fat: 24g
- Carbohydrates: 14g
- Protein: 9g

Kale and Apple Smoothie

Serving: 2

Prep Time: 5 minutes

Ingredients:

- 1 small stalk celery, chopped
- ¾ of kale, chopped, ribs and stem removed
- ½ banana
- ½ cup apple juice
- 1 tablespoon lemon juice

Directions:

1. Add all the listed ingredients to a blender

2. Blend on medium until you have a smooth

3. Serve chilled and enjoy!

Nutritional Contents:

- Calories: 100
- Fat: 9g
- Carbohydrates: 5g
- Protein: 1g

Almond and Kale Extreme

Serving: 1

Prep Time: 10 minutes

Ingredients:

- ¼ cup kale, torn
- 2 cups of water
- 2 ounces almonds
- 1 packet stevia, if you want
- ½ cup spinach, packed

Directions:

1. Soak almonds in water
2. Keep it overnight
3. Do not discard water and add all in the blender
4. Add all the listed ingredients to a blender
5. Blend on high until smooth and creamy
6. Enjoy your smoothie!

Nutritional Contents:

- Calories: 334
- Fat: 28g
- Carbohydrates: 14g
- Protein: 12g

Kale Mango Smoothie

Serving: 1

Prep Time: 10 minutes

Ingredients:

- 2 mangoes, peeled, pit removed and chopped
- 2 large bananas
- 4 tablespoons chia seeds
- 2 cups kale leaves
- 2 cups almond milk
- 2 cups of ice cubes

Directions:

1. Add all the listed ingredients to a blender
2. Blend until you have a smooth and creamy texture
3. Serve chilled and enjoy!

Nutritional Contents:

- Calories: 278
- Fat: 6.6g
- Carbohydrates: 55.2g
- Protein: 6.6g

Cranberry Beet

Serving: 2

Prep Time: 5 minutes

Ingredients:

- 1 ½ ounces baby kale
- 1 teaspoon pomegranate powder
- 3 tablespoons walnuts
- ½ inch ginger
- 1 tangerine, peeled
- 4 ounces beets, scrubbed and chopped
- 3 ounces cranberries

Directions:

1. Add all the listed ingredients to a blender

2. Blend until you have a smooth and creamy texture

3. Serve chilled and enjoy!

Nutritional Contents:

- Calories: 150
- Fat: 7g
- Carbohydrates: 18g
- Protein: 5g

Beetroot, Black Grape and Mint Smoothie

Serving: 2

Prep Time: 5 minutes

Ingredients:

- ½ cup beetroot, chopped
- 2 tablespoons lime juice
- 1 cup black grapes
- A handful of mint leaves
- A pinch of Himalayan pink salt

Directions:

1. Add all the listed ingredients to a blender
2. Blend until you have a smooth and creamy texture
3. Serve chilled and enjoy!

Nutritional Contents:

- Calories: 124
- Fat: 3g
- Carbohydrates: 18g
- Protein: 3g

Ginger Beet Detox Smoothie

Serving: 2

Prep Time: 10 minutes

Ingredients:

- 8 tablespoons beets, chopped
- 1 lemon, peeled
- ½ teaspoon wheatgrass
- ½ inch ginger, peeled
- 4 tablespoons mango, sliced
- 1 cup ice
- 1 cup of water

Directions:

1. Add all the listed ingredients to a blender
2. Blend until smooth
3. Serve chilled and enjoy!

Nutritional Contents:

- Calories: 42
- Fat: 0g
- Carbohydrates: 10g
- Protein: 1g

Chapter 12: Low-Fat Smoothies

The Great Shamrock Shake

Serving: 1

Prep Time: 10 minutes

Ingredients:

- 1 cup coconut milk, unsweetened
- 1 avocado, peeled, pitted and sliced
- 1 tablespoon pure vanilla extract
- 1 teaspoon pure peppermint extract
- Liquid stevia
- 1 cup ice

Directions:

1. Add all the listed ingredients into your blender
2. Blend until smooth
3. Serve chilled and enjoy!

Nutritional Contents:

- Calories: 195
- Fat: 19g
- Carbohydrates: 4.4g
- Protein: 2g

Chai Coconut Shake

Serving: 1

Prep Time: 10 minutes

Ingredients:

- ¼ cup shredded coconut, unsweetened
- 1 cup coconut milk, unsweetened
- 1 tablespoon pure vanilla extract
- 2 tablespoons almond butter
- 1 teaspoon ginger, grounded
- 1 teaspoon cinnamon, grounded
- 1 tablespoon flaxseed, grounded
- 5 ice cubes
- Pinch of allspice

Directions:

1. Add listed ingredients to a blender
2. Blend until you have a smooth and creamy texture
3. Serve chilled and enjoy!

Nutritional Contents:

- Calories: 233
- Fat: 20g
- Carbohydrates: 5g
- Protein: 4g

Apple, Dried Figs and Lemon Smoothie

Serving: 2

Prep Time: 5 minutes

Ingredients:

- 2 medium apples
- ¼ lemon
- A pinch of Himalayan pink salt
- 1 fig, dried

Directions:

1. Wash the apples, remove the pit and then roughly chop them
2. Chop the dried fig
3. Toss the chopped apples and figs into your blender
4. Add lemon juice and stir
5. Add a pinch of Himalayan pink salt
6. Serve chilled and enjoy!

Nutritional Contents:

- Calories: 120
- Fat: 2g
- Carbohydrates: 25g
- Protein: 5g

Almond Butter Smoothie

Serving: 2

Prep Time: 10 minutes

Ingredients:

- 3 cups nut milk, unsweetened
- 4 tablespoons almond butter
- 1 teaspoon cinnamon
- 2 scoops collagen peptides
- 4 tablespoons golden flax meal
- ¼ teaspoon salt
- ¼ teaspoon almond extract
- 12 ice cubes
- Liquid stevia, to taste

Directions:

1. Add all the listed ingredients to a blender
2. Blend until you have a smooth and creamy texture
3. Serve chilled and enjoy!

Nutritional Contents:

- Calories: 230
- Fat: 14.3g
- Carbohydrates: 8.9g
- Protein: 18.5g

Orange Banana Smoothie

Serving: 2

Prep Time: 10 minutes

Ingredients:

- 4 oranges, peeled and seeded
- 4 bananas
- 1 2-inch piece ginger root
- 2 carrots
- 2 cups of water

Directions:

1. Add all the listed ingredients to a blender

2. Blend until you have a smooth and creamy texture

3. Serve chilled and enjoy!

Nutritional Contents:

- Calories: 164
- Fat: 0.4g
- Carbohydrates: 28g
- Protein: 7.6g

Sage Blackberry

Serving: 2

Prep Time: 5 minutes

Ingredients:

- 1-ounce blackberries
- 3 tablespoons cashew
- 1 pear, chopped
- 4 ounces pineapple
- 3 sage leaves
- ½ teaspoon maqui berry powder

Directions:

1. Add all the listed ingredients to a blender

2. Blend until you have a smooth and creamy texture

3. Serve chilled and enjoy!

Nutritional Contents:

- Calories: 154
- Fat: 6g
- Carbohydrates: 24g
- Protein: 3g

Mini Pepper Popper Smoothie

Serving: 2

Prep Time: 5 minutes

Ingredients:

- 5 ounces mini peppers, seeded
- 4 ounces pineapple
- 1 orange, peeled
- 3 tablespoons almonds
- ½ lemon, juiced
- 1 cup of water
- 1 teaspoon rose hip powder

Directions:

1. Add all the listed ingredients to a blender

2. Blend until you have a smooth and creamy texture

3. Serve chilled and enjoy!

Nutritional Contents:

- Calories: 190
- Fat: 8g
- Carbohydrates: 21g
- Protein: 5g

Carrot, Watermelon and Cumin Smoothie

Serving: 2

Prep Time: 5 minutes

Ingredients:

- ½ cup carrot, chopped
- ½ teaspoon cumin powder
- 1 cup watermelon, seeded
- A pinch of Himalayan pink salt

Directions:

1. Add all the listed ingredients to a blender

2. Blend until you have a smooth and creamy texture

3. Serve chilled and enjoy!

Nutritional Contents:

- Calories: 112
- Fat: 1.2g
- Carbohydrates: 23g
- Protein: 6g

Papaya, Lemon and Cayenne Pepper Smoothie

Serving: 2

Prep Time: 5 minutes

Ingredients:

- 2 cups papaya
- ½ teaspoon cayenne pepper
- 3 tablespoons lemon juice

Directions:

1. Add all the listed ingredients to a blender
2. Blend until you have a smooth and creamy texture
3. Serve chilled and enjoy!

Nutritional Contents:

- Calories: 121
- Fat: 6g
- Carbohydrates: 20g
- Protein: 4g

Ginger Cantaloupe Detox Smoothie

Serving: 2

Prep Time: 10 minutes

Ingredients:

- 1 cantaloupe, sliced
- ½ inch ginger, peeled
- 1 tablespoon flaxseed
- 1 pear, chopped
- 1 cup of water
- 1 cup ice

Directions:

1. Add all the listed ingredients to a blender except the ginger

2. Blend until smooth

3. Then add ginger and blend again

4. Serve chilled and enjoy!

Nutritional Contents:

- Calories: 85
- Fat: 2g
- Carbohydrates: 19g
- Protein: 2g

Chapter 13: Protein Smoothies

Glorious Cinnamon Roll Smoothie

Serving: 1

Prep Time: 10 minutes

Ingredients:

- 1 cup unsweetened almond milk
- ½ teaspoon cinnamon
- ¼ teaspoon vanilla extract
- 1 tablespoon chia seeds
- 2 tablespoons vanilla protein powder
- 1 cup ice cubs

Directions:

1. Add all the listed ingredients into your blender

2. Blend until smooth

3. Serve chilled and enjoy!

Nutritional Contents:

- Calories: 145
- Fat: 4g
- Carbohydrates: 1.6g
- Protein: 0.6g

Blueberry and Avocado Smoothie

Serving: 1

Prep Time: 10 minutes

Ingredients:

- 1/4 cup frozen blueberries, unsweetened
- ½ avocado, peeled, pitted and sliced
- 1 cup unsweetened milk, vanilla
- 1 scoop coconut Zero Carb protein powder
- 1 tablespoon heavy cream
- Liquid stevia

Directions:

1. Add all the listed ingredients into your blender

2. Blend until smooth

3. Serve chilled and enjoy!

Nutritional Contents:

- Calories: 372
- Fat: 22g
- Carbohydrates: 4g
- Protein: 32g

The Great Avocado and Almond Delight

Serving: 1

Prep Time: 10 minutes

Ingredients:

- ½ avocado, peeled, pitted and sliced
- ½ cup almond milk, vanilla and unsweetened
- ½ teaspoon vanilla extract
- ½ cup half and half
- 1 tablespoon almond butter
- 1 scoop Zero Carb protein powder
- Pinch of cinnamon
- 2-4 ice cubes
- Liquid stevia

Directions:

1. Add all the listed ingredients into your blender

2. Blend until smooth

3. Serve chilled and enjoy!

Nutritional Contents:

- Calories: 252
- Fat: 18g
- Carbohydrates: 5g
- Protein: 17g

Subtle Raspberry Smoothie

Serving: 1

Prep Time: 10 minutes

Ingredients:

- ½ cup raspberries
- 1 scoop vanilla whey protein powder
- 1 scoop prebiotic fiber
- 1 cup unsweetened almond milk, vanilla
- 2 tablespoons coconut oil
- ¼ cup coconut flakes, unsweetened
- 3-4 ice cubes

Directions:

1. Add all the listed ingredients into your blender
2. Blend until smooth
3. Serve chilled and enjoy!

Nutritional Contents:

- Calories: 258
- Fat: 22g
- Carbohydrates: 7g
- Protein: 14g

Green Protein Smoothie

Serving: 2

Prep Time: 10 minutes

Ingredients:

- 2 bananas
- 4 cups mixed greens
- 2 tablespoons almond butter
- 1 cup almond milk, unsweetened

Directions:

1. Add all the listed ingredients to a blender
2. Blend until you have a smooth and creamy texture
3. Serve chilled and enjoy!

Nutritional Contents:

- Calories: 230
- Fat: 5.8g
- Carbohydrates: 39.5g
- Protein: 7.8g

Dark Chocolate Peppermint Smoothie

Serving: 2

Prep Time: 10 minutes

Ingredients:

- 2 large bananas, frozen
- 2 scoops chocolate protein powder
- 4 tablespoons cocoa powder
- 2 cups almond milk
- 2 pinches sea salt
- ½ teaspoon peppermint extract
- 4 large ice cubes
- 1 tablespoon dark chocolate chips for garnishing

Directions:

1. Add all the listed ingredients to a blender
2. Blend until you have a smooth and creamy texture
3. Serve chilled and enjoy!

Nutritional Contents:

- Calories: 132
- Fat: 2.6g
- Carbohydrates: 23.8g
- Protein: 7.2g

Very Creamy Green Machine

Serving: 1

Prep Time: 10 minutes

Ingredients:

- ½ cup frozen blueberries, unsweetened
- ½ avocado, peeled, pitted and sliced
- ½ cup unsweetened almond milk, vanilla
- ½ cup half and half
- 1 cup spinach
- 2-4 ice cubes
- 1 tablespoon almond butter
- 1 scoop Zero Carb protein powder
- 1 pack stevia

Directions:

1. Add listed ingredients to a blender
2. Blend until you have a smooth and creamy texture
3. Serve chilled and enjoy!

Nutritional Contents:

- Calories: 279
- Fat: 18g
- Carbohydrates: 9g
- Protein: 18g

The Cacao Super Smoothie

Serving: 1

Prep Time: 10 minutes

Ingredients:

- ½ avocado, peeled, pitted, sliced
- ½ cup frozen blueberries, unsweetened
- ½ cup almond milk, vanilla, unsweetened
- ½ cup half and half
- 1 scoop whey vanilla protein powder
- 1 tablespoon cacao powder
- Liquid stevia

Directions:

1. Add listed ingredients to a blender
2. Blend until you get a smooth and creamy texture
3. Serve chilled and enjoy!

Nutritional Contents:

- Calories: 445
- Fat: 14g
- Carbohydrates: 9g
- Protein: 16g

Healthy Chocolate Milkshake

Serving: 2

Prep Time: 10 minutes

Ingredients:

- 1 Scoop Whey isolate chocolate protein powder
- 16 ounces unsweetened almond milk, vanilla
- 1 pack stevia
- ½ cup crushed ice

Directions:

1. Add all the listed ingredients to a blender

2. Blend until you have a smooth and creamy texture

3. Serve chilled and enjoy!

Nutritional Contents:

- Calories: 292
- Fat: 25g
- Carbohydrates: 4g
- Protein: 15g

Cinnamon Protein Smoothie

Serving: 1

Prep Time: 10 minutes

Ingredients:

- 2 cups almond milk, unsweetened
- 2 scoops protein powder
- 2 teaspoons cinnamon
- 2 tablespoons almond butter
- 6 carrots, shredded
- 1 avocado, flesh only

Directions:

1. Add all the listed ingredients to a blender

2. Blend until you have a smooth and creamy texture

3. Serve chilled and enjoy!

Nutritional Contents:

- Calories: 362
- Fat: 22.7g
- Carbohydrates: 8g
- Protein: 20g

Chapter 14: Weight Loss Smoothies

The Fat Burner Espresso Smoothie

Serving: 2

Prep Time: 10 minutes

Ingredients:

- ¼ cup Greek yogurt, full fat
- 1 scoop Isopure Zero Carb protein powder
- 1 espresso shot
- 5 ice cubes
- Liquid stevia to sweeten
- Pinch of cinnamon

Directions:

1. Add listed ingredients to a blender
2. Blend until you have a smooth and creamy texture
3. Serve chilled and enjoy!

Nutritional Contents:

- Calories: 270
- Fat: 16g
- Carbohydrates: 2g
- Protein: 30g

Blueberry Crumble Smoothie

Serving: 2

Prep Time: 5 minutes

Ingredients:

- 1 apple, chopped
- 1 teaspoon acai berry powder
- 1 ounce blueberries
- 1 yellow squash, chopped
- 1 cup of water
- 1 cup ice
- 3 tablespoons walnuts

Directions:

1. Add all the listed ingredients to a blender
2. Blend until you have a smooth and creamy texture
3. Serve chilled and enjoy!

Nutritional Contents:

- Calories: 128
- Fat: 8g
- Carbohydrates: 14g
- Protein: 4g

Pumpkin Pie Buttered Coffee

Serving: 1

Prep Time: 10 minutes

Ingredients:

- 2 tablespoons pumpkin, canned
- 12 ounces hot coffee
- ¼ teaspoon pumpkin pie spice
- 1 tablespoon regular butter, unsalted
- Liquid stevia, to sweetened

Directions:

1. Add all the listed ingredients to a blender

2. Blend until you have a smooth and creamy texture

3. Serve chilled and enjoy!

Nutritional Contents:

- Calories: 120
- Fat: 12g
- Carbohydrates: 2g
- Protein: 1g

Healthy Raspberry and Coconut Glass

Serving: 1

Prep Time: 10 minutes

Ingredients:

- ¼ cup raspberries
- 1 tablespoon pepitas
- 1 tablespoon coconut oil
- ½ cup of coconut milk
- 1 cup 50/50 salad mix
- 1 ½ cups of water
- 1 pack stevia

Directions:

1. Add listed ingredients to a blender
2. Blend until you have a smooth and creamy texture
3. Serve chilled and enjoy!

Nutritional Contents:

- Calories: 408
- Fat: 41g
- Carbohydrates: 10g
- Protein: 5g

Banana, Almond, and Dark Chocolate Smoothie

Serving: 2

Prep Time: 5 minutes

Ingredients:

- 1 cup banana, sliced
- 4 tablespoons dark chocolate, grated 80% cocoa
- 8 almonds, soaked overnight
- ½ cup milk, low-fat and chilled

Directions:

1. Toss the sliced bananas, grated dark chocolate, almonds, and chilled milk
2. Add all the listed ingredients to a blender
3. Blend until you have a smooth and creamy texture
4. Serve chilled and enjoy!

Nutritional Contents:

- Calories: 114
- Fat: 1g
- Carbohydrates: 22g
- Protein: 5g

Kale Celery Smoothie

Serving: 2

Prep Time: 10 minutes

Ingredients:

- 3 cups kale, chopped
- 2 stalks celery, diced
- 1 red apple, cored and diced
- 2 cups almond milk, unsweetened
- 1 ¼ cups ice
- 2 teaspoons honey
- 2 tablespoons flaxseed, ground

Directions:

1. Add all the listed ingredients to a blender
2. Blend until you have a smooth and creamy texture
3. Serve chilled and enjoy!

Nutritional Contents:

- Calories: 341
- Fat: 29.8g
- Carbohydrates: 18.6g
- Protein: 5.3g

Kale Strawberry Smoothie

Serving: 2

Prep Time: 10 minutes

Ingredients:

- 2 cups kale, chopped
- 2 bananas
- 2 cups strawberries
- 2 cups ice
- 2 cups yogurt

Directions:

1. Add all the listed ingredients to a blender

2. Blend until you have a smooth and creamy texture

3. Serve chilled and enjoy!

Nutritional Contents:

- Calories: 358
- Fat: 3.8g
- Carbohydrates: 62.3g
- Protein: 18.2g

Carrot Coconut Smoothie

Serving: 2

Prep Time: 5 minutes

Ingredients:

- 6 ounces carrots, chopped
- 1 orange, peeled
- 4 ounces pineapple
- 1 teaspoon Camu Camu
- 2 tablespoons coconut flakes
- 1 cup ice
- 1 cup of water

Directions:

1. Add all the listed ingredients to a blender

2. Blend until you have a smooth and creamy texture

3. Serve chilled and enjoy!

Nutritional Contents:

- Calories: 140
- Fat: 2g
- Carbohydrates: 29g
- Protein: 2g

Mango Strawberry Smoothie

Serving: 1

Prep Time: 10 minutes

Ingredients:

- 1 cup Greek yogurt
- 2 mangoes, peeled, pit removed and chopped
- 4 teaspoons honey
- 3 cups strawberries, fresh or frozen
- 16 ice cubes

Directions:

1. Add all the listed ingredients to a blender
2. Blend until you have a smooth and creamy texture
3. Serve chilled and enjoy!

Nutritional Contents:

- Calories: 394
- Fat: 3.3g
- Carbohydrates: 85.4g
- Protein: 12.8g

The Blueberry and Chocolate Delight

Serving: 1

Prep Time: 10 minutes

Ingredients:

- ¼ cup blackberries
- 2 tablespoons Macadamia nuts, chopped
- ½ cup whole milk yogurt
- 1 tablespoon Dutch Processed Cocoa Powder
- 1 pack stevia
- 1 tablespoon MCT oil
- 1 ½ cups of water

Directions:

1. Add listed ingredients to a blender
2. Blend until you have a smooth and creamy texture
3. Serve chilled and enjoy!

Nutritional Contents:

- Calories: 463
- Fat: 43g
- Carbohydrates: 17g
- Protein: 9g

Chapter 15: Kid-Friendly Smoothies

Delish Pineapple and Coconut Milk Smoothie

Serving: 2

Prep Time: 5 minutes

Ingredients:

- ¾ cup of coconut water
- ¼ cup pineapple, frozen

Directions:

1. Add listed ingredients to a blender
2. Blend on high until you have a smooth and creamy texture
3. Serve chilled and enjoy!

Nutritional Contents:

- Calories: 132
- Fat: 12g
- Carbohydrates: 7g
- Protein: 1g

Pineapple Banana Smoothie

Serving: 2

Prep Time: 10 minutes

Ingredients:

- 2 apples
- 4 cups spinach
- 2 bananas
- 2 cups pineapples
- 2 cups of water

Directions:

1. Add all the listed ingredients to a blender

2. Blend until you have a smooth and creamy texture

3. Serve chilled and enjoy!

Nutritional Contents:

- Calories: 317
- Fat: 1.2g
- Carbohydrates: 81.6g
- Protein: 4.5g

Nutella Lovers Smoothie

Serving: 4

Prep Time: 10 minutes

Ingredients:

- 2 cups pear, ripped and chopped
- ½ cup roasted, unsalted hazelnuts
- 3 cups of coconut water
- 4 tablespoons cocoa powder, unsalted
- 4 Medjool dates pitted
- 3 teaspoons vanilla extract
- 4 cups ice

Directions:

1. Add all the listed ingredients to a blender

2. Blend until you have a smooth and creamy texture

3. Serve chilled and enjoy!

Nutritional Contents:

- Calories: 301
- Fat: 6.9g
- Carbohydrates: 59.8g
- Protein: 5g

Cocoa Banana Smoothie

Serving: 4

Prep Time: 10 minutes

Ingredients:

- 4 large bananas, peeled and sliced
- ½ cup creamy peanut butter
- 2 cups almond milk
- 4 tablespoons cocoa powder, unsweetened
- 1 teaspoon vanilla extract
- 2 cups ice

Directions:

1. Add all the listed ingredients to a blender

2. Blend until you have a smooth and creamy texture

3. Serve chilled and enjoy!

Nutritional Contents:

- Calories: 346
- Fat: 17.4g
- Carbohydrates: 46.1g
- Protein: 10g

Maple Chocolate Smoothie

Serving: 2

Prep Time: 10 minutes

Ingredients:

- 4 tablespoons cocoa powder
- 2 ½ cups of almond milk
- 1 cup oats, rolled
- 1 teaspoon vanilla extract
- 1 tablespoon maple syrup
- 2 tablespoons almond butter

Directions:

1. Add all the listed ingredients to a blender

2. Blend until you have a smooth and creamy texture

3. Serve chilled and enjoy!

Nutritional Contents:

- Calories: 170
- Fat: 7.2g
- Carbohydrates: 23.8g
- Protein: 5.6g

Raw Chocolate Smoothie

Serving: 2

Prep Time: 10 minutes

Ingredients:

- 2 medium bananas
- 4 tablespoons peanut butter, raw
- 1 cup almond milk
- 3 tablespoons cocoa powder, raw
- 2 tablespoons honey, raw

Directions:

1. Add all the listed ingredients to a blender
2. Blend until you have a smooth and creamy texture
3. Serve chilled and enjoy!

Nutritional Contents:

- Calories: 217
- Fat: 2.8g
- Carbohydrates: 52.7g
- Protein: 3.4g

Dark Chocolate Chia Smoothie

Serving: 2

Prep Time: 10 minutes

Ingredients:

- 6 tablespoons chia seeds
- 4 tablespoons cocoa powder, unsweetened
- 2 bananas, peeled
- 2 cups spinach, raw
- 2 cups almond milk
- 1 teaspoon vanilla extract

Directions:

1. Add all the listed ingredients to a blender
2. Blend until you have a smooth and creamy texture
3. Serve chilled and enjoy!

Nutritional Contents:

- Calories: 362
- Fat: 29.1g
- Carbohydrates: 27.4g
- Protein: 7.5g

Apple Berry Smoothie

Serving: 2

Prep Time: 10 minutes

Ingredients:

- 2 large apples
- 4 cups spinach
- 2 cups berries, mixed
- 2 cups of water

Directions:

1. Add all the listed ingredients to a blender

2. Blend until you have a smooth and creamy texture

3. Serve chilled and enjoy!

Nutritional Contents:

- Calories: 210
- Fat: 1.1g
- Carbohydrates: 50g
- Protein: 3.3g

Minty Chocolate Smoothie

Serving: 3

Prep Time: 10 minutes

Ingredients:

- 4 tablespoons cocoa powder
- 2 cups almond milk
- 2 bananas, frozen
- 1 2/3 cups spinach leaves
- ½ cup mint leaves
- Stevia liquid, to taste

Directions:

1. Add all the listed ingredients to a blender
2. Blend until you have a smooth and creamy texture
3. Serve chilled and enjoy!

Nutritional Contents:

- Calories: 352
- Fat: 29.7g
- Carbohydrates: 25.3g
- Protein: 5.2g

Chocolate Spinach Smoothie

Serving: 4

Prep Time: 10 minutes

Ingredients:

- 4 cups banana, sliced
- 2 cups spinach, packed
- 6 tablespoons peanut butter
- 2 cups almond milk
- ½ cup of cocoa powder
- 2 tablespoons flaxseeds, grounded

Directions:

1. Add all the listed ingredients to a blender

2. Blend until you have a smooth and creamy texture

3. Serve chilled and enjoy!

Nutritional Contents:

- Calories: 356
- Fat: 16.2g
- Carbohydrates: 51.7g
- Protein: 13g

Conclusion

I am honored to think that you found my book interesting and informative enough to read it all through to the end.

I heartily thank you for purchasing my book, and I do hope that it helped you understand the fundamentals of Smoothie making and how to utilize it to the fullest potential.

I bid you farewell in your Smoothie Journey, stay safe and God Bless!

Made in the USA
Monee, IL
21 January 2021